THE CONSCIOUS PARENT'S GUIDE TO

Positive Discipline

A mindful approach for building a healthy, respectful relationship with your child

Jennifer Costa

A adamsmedia

Avon, Massachusetts

DEDICATION

For Annie and Alex, who make me proud to be a parent, and to Jimmy, who is a never-ending source of support and perspective.

Published by
Adams Media, a division of F+W Media, Inc.
57 Littlefield Street, Avon, MA 02322. U.S.A.
www.adamsmedia.com

Contains material adapted from *The Everything® Parent's Guide to Positive Discipline, 2nd Edition* by Ellen Bowers, copyright © 2011, 2004 by F+W Media, Inc., ISBN 10: 1-4405-2850-0, ISBN 13: 978-1-4405-2850-7 and *The Everything® Parent's Guide to Raising Mindful Children* by Jeremy Wardle and Maureen Weinhardt, copyright © 2013 by F+W Media, Inc., ISBN 10: 1-4405-6130-3, ISBN 13: 978-1-4405-6130-6.

ISBN 10: 1-4405-9435-X
ISBN 13: 978-1-4405-9435-9
eISBN 10: 1-4405-9436-8
eISBN 13: 978-1-4405-9436-6

Printed in the United States of America.

10   9   8   7   6   5   4   3   2   1

Cover design by Alexandra Artiano.

This book is available at quantity discounts for bulk purchases.
For information, please call 1-800-289-0963.

Contents

Introduction

Being a conscious parent requires more than just offering caregiving. Conscious parenting is a nurturing and educational process that allows you to build strong bonds and help your child develop from a completely dependent infant to an independent, self-confident adult. Nurturing is a matter of expressing love. Education is a matter of training. Balanced parents offer a healthy mix of love and training. Providing one or the other is not enough.

As a parent, discipline is your responsibility. Your job involves helping your child develop appropriate beliefs and behaviors as a result of your example and guidance. The definition of right and wrong in your family depends on the values that you carry into parenthood from your own background and experiences. No two families are the same when it comes to beliefs and standards.

Becoming a first-time parent can be a humbling experience. It's easy to feel overwhelmed and think that you don't have what it takes to raise a child. The truth is, children teach you how to parent as they grow. Chances are, you know more than you think you do. Here are six "As" that most children want from their parents as they grow up.

- Attention—active listening and noticing
- Acceptance—understanding and acknowledgment
- Approval—valuing and praise
- Appreciation—recognition and thanks
- Affection—love through telling and through touch
- Authority—rules and guidelines for living

Take a deep breath, believe in yourself, deliver these, and you'll do just fine.

CHAPTER 1

Conscious Parenting

Conscious parenting is all about building strong bonds with your children through mindfulness, positivity, and awareness. Traditional authoritarian techniques cause diminished confidence and frequent conflict. Conscious parenting, however, promotes a positive emotional connection with your child. By acknowledging your child's uniqueness, you have the power to create a safe environment where she feels understood and heard. Conscious parenting focuses on positive discipline, active modeling, and the search for peaceful solutions. This approach benefits all children, especially those who are easily frustrated or often feel they have little control over their own behavior. Adopting the conscious parent philosophy can also relieve your stress and improve your child's confidence. Building a strong bond and mutual respect will encourage positive behavior patterns.

The Benefits of Conscious Parenting

Conscious parenting isn't a set of rules or regulations that you must follow, but rather a belief system. Conscious parents engage and connect with their children, using mindful and positive discipline rather than punishment. Your complete presence, without distraction, builds a child's confidence and promotes mutual understanding. The most important component of conscious parenting is the establishment of a deep emotional connection with your child so you can understand the underlying reasons for behavior.

> Conscious parenting is about active listening and embracing a nonjudgmental acceptance of yourself and your child. As you engage in the act of *becoming*, you will discover a heightened sense of emotional awareness of yourself and your child and a greater compassion for yourself and your child.

The benefits of conscious parenting include improved communication, a stronger bond with your child, and peaceful resolutions. Some of these benefits appear immediately, while others take time to emerge. The benefits of conscious parenting and mindfulness are a result of making this philosophy a part of your daily life. With practice, conscious parenting becomes an integral part of who you are, and can then become a central part of who your child is as well.

SELF-AWARENESS AND SELF-CONTROL

Through conscious parenting you will develop a heightened awareness of yourself and your inner being, including your emotions, thoughts, and behaviors. As you become more aware of these influencing forces, you can begin to acknowledge them without being at their mercy. For example, when you are aware that you are becoming angry, you have a choice to act or to acknowledge that feeling directly. You will begin to notice the things that tend to set you off—your triggers—and be able to anticipate your emotions before they take hold of you. Your child will witness your behavior and be likely to emulate it.

Mindfulness is the practice of being attentive in every moment, and noticing what is taking place both inside and outside of you without passing judgment. It is the practice of purposefully acknowledging your thoughts, emotions, experiences, and surroundings as they arise.

As you become more skilled at acknowledging your thoughts and feelings, you will begin to notice them more quickly, and allow them to have less control over your actions. Self-awareness is a powerful tool. It opens up the possibility of saying, "Hey, I'm pretty mad right now . . ." as opposed to screaming at somebody you care about because you were upset about something else. It can provide the same benefit for your child, helping him to communicate his feelings rather than react from a place of emotion. As with most things, children learn this best by seeing it modeled by the adults in their lives.

WELL-BEING

Conscious parents understand that all they do and say over the course of each day matters. As you become more mindful, you might find that you become more accepting of those things in life that you can't change. This sense of well-being offers a satisfaction and contentment in knowing that you are who you are intended to be, doing precisely what you are designed for in the moment.

EMPATHY

The awareness you gain as a conscious parent has the practical purpose of redefining your perception of yourself and your compassionate understanding of your child. When you understand how your child experiences the world and how he learns, you can communicate in ways that really reach him. Conscious parenting encourages you to view your behavior through your child's point of view and to mold your reactions to meet his needs. This largely happens through modeling, or teaching by positive example. Doing so allows you to pass on the values that are important to you.

Everyone possesses the tools for contributing something of value. Assess your gifts and talents—those personality traits and skills that make you unique—and determine how to employ them to enhance your parenting. If you take a full account of yourself—good, bad, and indifferent—and *own* the sum total of your individual experience, you are taking the first step toward conscious parenting.

ACCEPTANCE AND VALIDATION

Your child relies upon you and your family to provide a solid foundation of self-esteem. Equipped with a strong sense of self-worth, your child will be better prepared to face life's challenges. Much of your time and energy will be expended in raising, counseling, and disciplining your child in ways that he will understand. It is important to equalize those occasions by reinforcing your love and appreciation of his gifts and talents.

Giving Your Child Your Full Attention

All too often parents multitask their way through the day. This is a coping mechanism you have probably developed as a means of juggling the many projects, tasks, errands, and obligations that you are responsible for. Although it is a common approach to managing a busy day, it divides your attention and distracts your mind.

To avoid this becoming an issue between you and your child (and to make sure you're modeling the kind of focus and engagement you want your child to use as well), practice engaged listening when you are with your family. This means minimizing distractions, making eye contact, and giving the speaker (in this case, your child) your full attention.

Even if you set down what you are doing and are looking at your child, you might not be fully engaged. Is your mind focused on what she is saying, or is it still planning, scheduling, remembering, projecting, or worrying? It is very easy to only half-listen, and this can be especially true when it comes to listening to children.

> Multitasking is neurologically impossible. When you multitask, you are actually rapidly switching between tasks. Each time you do so, you lose efficiency and concentration. Do one thing at a time so you can use your whole brain.

The stories your child tells are not always relevant to your adult concerns. The idea behind active listening is not to suddenly care about what everyone else brought to school for Show and Tell today; it's about understanding what's important to your child and acknowledging her experiences. Active discussions build strong bonds. When a person you love cares about something, it becomes easier to see that "something" through her eyes and come to appreciate it all the more.

Understanding Behavior

Conscious parenting is about viewing behavior from a standpoint of "why." When you understand the reasoning behind the behavior, it is easier to react in a way that will benefit your child.

Many times, a child's behavior is the result of a deep-rooted emotional concern. Being present with your child will help you to identify the reasons for specific behaviors and sense triggers. By encouraging your child to express his emotions verbally, rather than react through inappropriate behavior, you are teaching your child valuable self-regulation methods that will help him to be a well-functioning, confident, and empathetic adult.

Understanding your child's behavior is not a process that happens overnight. Getting to the root of a behavior involves active, engaged listening.

Discussing problem behaviors in the heat of the moment will accomplish little. Teaching coping strategies that will allow for peaceful resolution and, later, conversation about the feelings surrounding a specific behavior is a key strategy in conscious parenting.

Important Points to Consider

As you develop conscious parenting skills, you will see a transformation in the relationship between you and your child. As you enhance your parenting techniques, keep the following things in mind:

- O Act deliberately. Take the time to really think before acting. What am I modeling by reacting the way that I do?

- O Speak and listen from your heart. Don't half-listen to your child. Be engaged and seek out information that will help you understand her better.

- O Be a positive example. Model the behavior that you'd like your child to emulate. Share your values through positive leadership.

- O Acknowledge your emotions and encourage your child to do the same. Recognize and accept the internal factors that result in behavior, both positive and negative.

 **CHAPTER 2**

The Basics of Discipline

Children are born totally dependent on the adults who care for them. Your job as a parent is to provide consistent support and nurturing love, and to create a foundation of beliefs and behavior that your child can live by. It is through positive discipline that you will create this foundation. For the conscious parent, discipline requires more than just getting your child to adhere to behavior norms; it means understanding and addressing the feelings underlying undesirable behaviors.

Conscious versus Unconscious Discipline

Discipline is the ongoing process of instruction and correction through which your children are taught to act within family rules and according to family values. Unconscious discipline focuses on the negative, and the desire to immediately correct that behavior. What it fails to consider is the root cause of a behavior. Conscious discipline does not simply address a behavior, but also the thoughts and feelings that led to that behavior.

> The most powerful way for parents to encourage positive behavior is to model that behavior and reward compliance with thoughtful appreciation, approval, or praise. A simple smile or hug can do wonders for reinforcing positive behavior.

Athletic trainers know how to focus on conscious, positive discipline. For a champion athlete to remain a champion, he has to stay focused on what he's doing right. Certainly the athlete wants to know when he's doing something wrong, so he can fix it. But fixating on the negative is a great mistake. Have you ever been shouted at or humiliated by a coach? You may not even remember why, but you can certainly remember the negative feelings. Positive discipline focuses on what is going right and keeps a consistent focus on what needs to be continued. Conscious discipline incorporates the "why" that led to the positive. If targeted stretching or practice drills led to increased performance, these activities are acknowledged and encouraged. The same principle applies when it comes to parents training their child.

How Discipline Affects Your Relationship

Consider your own behavior. How often do you give rewards versus punishment? Children are pleasure-seeking, so they tend to repeat behaviors that are rewarded. Even a small amount of praise will increase the likelihood that a behavior is repeated in the future. Children are also pain-avoiding, so they're not likely to repeat a behavior that is appropriately punished. Does your child continue to repeat a behavior that you've consistently punished? If you're providing attention, even the negative kind, you might be inadvertently rewarding a behavior by not acknowledging the root cause. Also consider that your frustration can lead to inappropriate responses. When you provide discipline, are you responding to your child's behavior, or your feelings?

INFLUENCE OVER TIME

Initially, rewards and punishments seem equally influential. Over time, repeated use of both methods will reveal significant differences in the influence they have on a child. The stronger the bond is between parent and child, the more likely cooperation is to happen. When a relationship becomes negative, resentment can occur, leading to decreased compliance. When punishment is expected, the desire to try is taken away.

> Positive or negative discipline treatment from parents deeply affects how children learn to view themselves. Children who are praised often, and not judged harshly for their feelings, are more likely to grow up to be self-affirming, confident adults, but heavily criticized children often grow into negative, unconfident adults.

If you want your discipline to work well, make sure you consistently affirm a relationship that your child really values. Rely on instruction rather than correction, on affirmation rather than punishment, and on being positive rather than being negative.

Classical Conditioning in a Nutshell

Many parents are familiar with the concept of classical conditioning. When a reward is paired with a certain behavioral response, and this pattern is repeated consistently, the behavior becomes habit. If you give a child ten dollars each time he aces a test, soon he will consistently get stellar test grades. The flaw in this technique is that when the stimulus—in this case, the ten bucks—is suddenly removed, that positive behavior might cease.

The most powerful reinforcement is actually an intermittent reward. In other words, from time to time, acknowledge your child's positive behavior and reward it by giving a hug and saying thank you. Your child will begin to get the idea that this behavior is what you like to see.

COMPASSIONATE INSTRUCTION VERSUS CORRECTION

Each time your son or daughter breaks a rule, you are presented with an opportunity. Conscious parenting views discipline as a teaching process. Maybe your child doesn't understand what is being asked of him. Maybe the behavior is a logical response to a feeling that he is experiencing. Responding with clear, compassionate instruction will help you to get your point across, while strengthening your relationship.

An example of this might be: "The reason I've asked you to not tell people that I'm not home over the phone is that I don't want strangers to know you are here alone for a little while. Next time, please tell the person that I cannot come to the phone right now, and ask for a number I can call back." Sometimes a negative behavior is intentional, and a corrective response is in order. Explain how a behavior has made you feel and why it needs to stop. When the behavior is severe enough to warrant a consequence, make sure that the response is appropriate, not too harsh or too lenient, and that you respond this way consistently.

Do not use correction with a child who is genuinely not aware of a rule. This can lead to feelings of betrayal and mistrust. When your child does something inappropriate, turn this into a teachable experience. Hold your child accountable only for following the rules that you've clearly communicated to him.

When you correct a child, you should follow the correction with instruction, so he knows how to do things differently the next time. It's difficult for a child to correct a behavior when he doesn't know how he is supposed to react. Give clear examples describing what he can do differently next time.

Understanding Instruction

So how do you teach rules and values? Providing concise instruction and explaining why a rule is so important to you will ensure that your child knows what's expected of her.

PARENTS AS MODELS

As a parent, you are a family leader. What you do greatly impacts a child's view of the world. If you ask your child to stop doing something that you do consistently, you are sending a very confusing message. If you leave items lying around the house and then reprimand your child for not picking up her things, she will receive mixed messages. Hitting a child as a punishment for her hitting another child is simply not fair. This is teaching your child that it is her, and not the behavior, that you don't like.

Setting Examples

Modeling requires more than just instruction. If you want your children to demonstrate patience, exhibit patience. If you want your children to listen to you, listen to them. If you want your children to control their tempers, then control your own. If you truly value patience, listening, and temper control, then promote these values by displaying them.

By acknowledging and accepting your shortcomings and striving to correct them, you can use your mistakes to teach your children how to deal with challenges. It's okay that you're not perfect, and children need to understand that this is okay for them too.

Bad Habits

You might have a bad habit that you'd rather your child not develop. Suppose, despite your best efforts, you are frequently late, and now one of your children is starting a habit of keeping other people waiting. Could this behavior be the result of anxiety, which results in a self-fulfilling prophecy? It's completely acceptable to acknowledge this flaw, communicate it to your child, and work together to come up with a solution.

You have an enormous opportunity as a parent to teach by both instruction and modeling. Don't expect perfection from yourself or your child.

INSTRUCTIONAL AMNESIA

Adults often forget that not all behavior comes naturally. It can be difficult to identify with a child who seems to not be picking up something as quickly as you'd like her to. Think of how you feel when you have to learn a new software program. You might make many mistakes (and get very frustrated) while mastering the skills required. How behind do you feel, compared to your more tech-savvy spouse (or younger coworker), who seems to pick it up in half the time? Well, this is the way your child feels a lot of the time in comparison to you.

LEARNING BY REPEATING

It's easy to assume that children should learn something the first time it is taught, when this is usually not a realistic expectation. In most cases, children, like adults, are multiple-trial learners.

Reminding and repeating instruction is part of the parent's role. It is also important in determining which instructional approach works best with your child. Some children learn directions best from being shown the steps or from seeing a description in written words (visual). Some children learn directions best from being told and hearing it explained out loud (auditory). Other children learn from hands-on activity, having some physical involvement to help them understand (kinesthetic). Many elementary teachers use all three approaches to get information across. They put a homework assignment on the chalkboard for children to see, they read the assignment out loud for students to hear, and they ask students to write down the assignment in their notebooks to give students something to do.

Learning requires repetition. This often means providing instruction in multiple ways. If you give instructions one way to your child, and she repeats the offending behavior, be sure to explain your expectations differently the next time you correct her.

Principles of Positive Correction

Correction should be reserved for deliberate misbehavior, and it should be given with care. When an unnecessary correction takes place, it can threaten a young child's security and injure his self-esteem. Angry correction can cause your child to wonder if you are actually upset with him rather than the behavior.

The goal of correction is to get a positive behavior change from the child in a manner that addresses the root causes of this behavior.

Consider the five principles of correction.

O **Correct a child's behavior, but never degrade a child's person.** Don't say "You're a bad boy!" When you tell him that his behavior is unacceptable, he still needs to know that he himself is accepted by you. A bad behavior is not the result of a bad child. Children should never worry that they are at risk of losing your acceptance.

O **Don't give correction without instruction.** Correction can be confusing if an alternate behavior is not provided. Negative commands like "Stop that!" or "Don't do that!" lack instructional power. The child thinks, "I know my parent wants me to quit complaining, but I haven't been given an alternative."

O **Keep correction nonjudgmental.** When a behavior occurs, there is generally an underlying cause. Saying things like "You should have known better, I've told you a thousand times! You've really let me down!" only devalues a child who already realizes that a mistake has been made. Therefore, simply say, "I disagree with the choice you have made, here is why, and this is the consequence." Of course, there are some behaviors that have the potential to impact the safety of your child and those around him. For example, when a child lashes out physically, you'll need to intervene. In this case, once the situation is stable, explain that this behavior is forbidden, and while your love for your child has not diminished, dangerous behavior will not be tolerated.

O **Express appreciation for listening to and complying with the correction.** When a child responds appropriately to correction, acknowledge it! Accepting feedback is difficult, even for adults, and a sincere effort to change a behavior should be recognized.

O **End by reasserting expectations of cooperation after correction is over.** Unwanted behavior is likely to continue if a child doesn't understand what's expected of him. Let him know that you are his ally, and that allies work together to resolve problems. Always end correction on this reaffirming note: "I know you will do better the next time."

Correctional responses should be reasonable and rational. If you correct your child with anger, he may believe he is being corrected because you are angry, not because he displayed behavior that is unacceptable.

There should be a balance between instructional and correctional responses. If you constantly correct, then you have removed all positive incentives for cooperation. A child who believes that punishment is inevitable has no reason to change.

Behavior Snapshot

All children will make poor behavior choices. This is just a fact of life. But it is how you deal with this behavior that will influence the adults they become. For discipline to be effective and well-received by your child, it must be more instructional than corrective. If you choose a more punitive approach with restrictions and punishments, your child is more likely to continue the behaviors.

What happens: Your active seven-year-old consistently slams the screen door each time she runs in and out of the house. The loud noise jars you each time it happens and it's beginning to damage the door frame.

What you *want* to do: Scream "How many times have I told you not to slam that door?! What's wrong with you?"

What you should do: Calmly realize that she is not being willfully disobedient. She is enthusiastic about what she's doing and forgot what you said before. You have now acknowledged the underlying feelings that are causing the behavior. Instead of yelling about it, quietly take her by the hand and demonstrate how to close the door without making a bang.

Important Points to Consider

Providing discipline while enhancing the relationship with your child can be challenging, at best. As you develop your discipline strategy, consider the following points:

- Provide instruction. Give clear instruction to communicate rules and expectations. Understand that children learn best when you incorporate multiple learning styles into your instructions.

- Correct the behavior, not the child. It's important for your child to understand that even when you don't accept a behavior, you'll always accept him.

- Model good behavior while accepting that we all have flaws. Show your child what you'd like to see by modeling appropriate behavior. Understand that it's okay to make mistakes and explain to your child that neither of you is perfect.

 **CHAPTER 3**

Meeting the Challenges of Discipline

Learning to provide positive, instructional discipline takes patience and practice. Sometimes it seems easier to just do things for your child instead of telling her how to do it, but this does not yield long-term benefits. Providing thoughtful discipline is like making an investment in your child's future. Taking the time to teach to and understand your child will build a strong skill foundation while promoting a positive sense of self-worth.

Your Attitude Matters

Repeated discipline problems can lead to changes in your own behavior. When you consider your own outlook, remember that children have an uncanny way of identifying with your attitude rather than your words. Fatigue, frustration, and anger can have a huge impact on your outlook. Discipline problems can cause parents to:

○ **Develop a negative perception of the child:** "She was born to make trouble." (No child is born to make trouble.)

○ **Make generalizations about the child instead of identifying specifics:** "She has no respect for what I say!" (The child was simply arguing about not being allowed to have a snack before supper.)

○ **Narrow their perception of the child:** "All she ever does is wrong!" (The parent ignores all that the child does right.)

○ **Take situations personally:** "She must hate me, that's why she's arguing." (The child is too self-occupied to consider the effect of her arguing on others.)

○ **Feel helpless and hopeless:** "We've tried everything and nothing works!" (No parents have ever tried every technique; they have only grown tired and become too frustrated to stay consistent or to try anything else.)

When you become so fixated on the problem that your view of the child becomes negative, it's time to ask for support. Leaning on a friend or a support group can help you regain perspective.

It is possible to use discipline to promote a positive relationship. When you shift your thinking and view discipline as a teaching tool, your child will learn to accept her mistakes (and yours) and adapt to this new way of thinking.

Guidance for the Future

Your child can be viewed as an adult in training. In order to shape your child's future, you must be actively involved in the teaching process. The ultimate goal is to produce a happy, well-functioning adult, and to do so using positive discipline and nurturing support. This can sometimes be much easier than it sounds.

AVOIDING BAD HABITS

Whatever bad habits your child has developed by now are likely to be carried into the future if they are left unaddressed. Consider the underlying causes of these habits. Does using foul language make your child feel in control of a conversation? When administering discipline, also suggest an alternate behavior that can help your child cope with the root of the problem.

When your child develops a bad habit such as whining, encourage a replacement habit: "Practice asking me cheerfully, and you may have a better chance of getting what you want."

PROMOTING GOOD HABITS

Be thoughtful and intentional about the habits you want your child to practice now that will impact his future. For example, ask yourself what habits related to spiritual faith, character, integrity, nutrition, exercise, work, relaxation, play, personal organization, hygiene, health, communication, manners, responsibility, or service to others you want to teach. Then decide what specific activities you can encourage the child to do to help him develop these habits. For example, if you'd like to encourage your child to have a strong work ethic, you may encourage him to earn the things he wants by completing a task start to finish.

Remember that your modeling has a profound impact on your child's behavior, so allow him to see the positive impact of your own healthy habits.

Risking Resentment

When discipline is based on the principles of power and control, rather than purpose and instruction, gaps form, which can lead to resentment. Authoritarian parents expect their children to adhere to behavior standards that are often unachievable, so it's quite natural for children to push back or retreat into a cycle of resentment. When children view you as a coach, on the other hand, they approach situations with mutual respect in mind. Forceful discipline with the end goal of conformity can lead to your child viewing you as a dictator rather than a leader.

When negative demands are replaced with encouraging instruction, the risk of this parent/child rift formation decreases. This is not to say that you should expect a thank you each time you do provide discipline. Your child is, after all, human.

ACTS OF LOVE

When you discipline with the child's present and future welfare in mind, discipline becomes an act of love. If you are so inclined, you can explain this part of your parental responsibility to your child by saying something like this: "Please know that I care enough to instruct and correct you for your own good, even when it causes you to feel I am a mean parent, or to feel angry at me, and it causes friction between us. It's hard to face your disapproval when I raise issues you don't want to discuss. It's hard to make demands and set limits you resent when I take a stand for your best interests against what you want or like. But I love you enough to do so when I believe it is required. Discipline is not something I do to you; it is something I do for you."

At least in the moment, discipline can feel like thankless work. That's why taking a long view is important. In your child's adulthood, you will see some fruits of your steadfast labors to teach healthy habits. The child with whom you battled endless years to pick up a messy room emerges as a young person who likes to live in a clean and orderly space. The child who required your continued insistence to accomplish homework becomes a young person with a strong and reliable work ethic. And you will think to yourself, "Maybe my efforts were worthwhile after all!"

PRESSURE TO BE PERFECT

Many parents feel intense pressure to be "perfect." This can be harmful to you and your child. As a conscious parent, it's okay to acknowledge your own imperfections and teach your child to do the same. Each parent and child are unique individuals, and comparing your family to another is unfair. Placing pressure on yourself or your child to live up to what you perceive to be another person's standards not only creates resentment, it also diminishes self-esteem.

Striving for perfection can cause intense pressure. Nobody should feel that she must reach unreachable standards just to be okay.

Keeping Priorities in Order

Being a conscious parent means accepting and fulfilling your own needs, as well as those of your children. Allowing time for self-care is essential to being a centered parent. Even if your time is scarce, periodically make time to take a bubble bath, meditate, or head to bed a little early.

It is also important to put effort into adult relationships. Parents who stop nourishing their relationships with spouses, friends, and adult family members can become estranged and fractious with each other, which carries over into relationships with children.

Making your child your only priority is not fair to you or your child.

Partners can become so preoccupied with parenthood that they neglect to pay adequate attention to themselves and their relationship. This can actually have a negative effect on a child's development. Remember, your children are looking to you to model what appropriate relationships look like. When you neglect to care for yourself or your relationships, your child learns to do the same.

Behavior Snapshot

Discipline is not easy, but it does provide an opportunity for teaching. Try to keep discipline focused on positive development, rather than strict conformity. You do, after all, want your child to gain all of the tools he'll need to be successful in life.

What happens: Your teenage son requests a significant amount of money, even after you and he have worked out a budget for his expenses.

What you *want* to do: Give him the money, and be done with it.

What you should do: Encourage him to seek out short-term work situations that could bring in the cash he wants. Encourage him, saying that you trust he will find a way to solve the problem.

Important Points to Consider

Disciplining is never an easy process, but when it is done well, it can provide valuable life-lessons for your child. Here are some important points to consider:

- The attitude through which you approach discipline will determine the outcome.

- Exploring the root causes of negative behaviors will help you to prevent reoccurrence.

- By providing positive discipline, you are actually teaching your child problem-solving and communication skills that will allow him to be a more successful adult.

- Harsh, negative discipline can foster feelings of resentment and cause future behavioral problems.

- By viewing discipline as education, you can instill your positive values into your child.

CHAPTER 4

Understanding the Limits of Parental Control

There are many theories about parental influence (nurture) on a child's biologically determined personality (nature), and how this relates to parenting. The conscious parenting philosophy suggests that we should accept and acknowledge children's personality traits, while understanding that parental influence plays a valuable and important role in determining how a child will ultimately develop into adulthood.

Placing Parental Influence in Perspective

The act of parenting matters. However, many other factors also shape the course of a child's growth. Consider just a few sources of influence over which parents have no control.

- **The culture into which a child is born or the onslaught of media messages that it sends**—the experiences it glamorizes, the ideals it presents, and the motivations it encourages.

- **A child's inborn characteristics**—the temperament, personality, aptitudes, and physical traits that genetic inheritance endows.

- **The choices a child makes**—the personal decisions that ultimately determine what he will or will not do.

- **What a child experiences away from home**—the unfamiliar and challenging situations he experiences outside of the household.

- **A child's companions**—the opportunities for risk-taking, for experimenting with adventure, and for the forbidden that peers provide.

- **Chance events**—the play of luck that can favor, spare, or victimize a young person's life.

Since parenting is only one of the many influences on a child's development, how your child "turns out" is not all to your credit or blame. And, like it or not, many of the factors that influence the development of your child are simply out of your control.

Recognizing the Extent of Parental Responsibility

For you to accept total blame for anything and everything that your child experiences is placing too much power on parental influence. Expecting to have this much control over your children can lead to feelings of inappropriate guilt—parents punishing themselves for what they are powerless to control. Then the child, who cannot resist manipulating a guilty parent to escape personal responsibility, may declare, "It's not my fault for failing; it's yours for moving and making me change schools!" And the parent may believe it.

As a parent, you influence your child through modeling (who and how you are), treatment (how you choose to act and react with your child), structure (what you value and allow), and education (the information and instruction you provide).

It's okay to accept and appreciate that you are not all-powerful. No parent can completely protect or prepare her child, and mistakes are part of our humanness. Neither you nor your child will ever be able to achieve absolute perfection, and why would you want to?

To Change Your Child, Change Yourself

Realizing the profound effect that your behavior has on the healthy development of your child is the first step to teaching through modeling. Try lowering your voice to de-escalate your anger, and, in time, your child will follow suit. The same holds true with acceptance. As you acknowledge your own oneness, your child will learn to accept his own unique traits.

Often, asking a child to do something works better than telling him to do it, because the asking fosters respect. Asking is a courtesy that acknowledges the child's choice and encourages cooperation. Unfortunately, some children do not respond well to asking and, in this case, giving clear, positive direction may be more effective.

GETTING OUT OF NEGATIVE CYCLES

If you find yourself repeatedly in a spot where you and your child are angry with each other, this is one sign that you are trapped in an unconscious, self-defeating pattern.

What can you do to try to gain your child's cooperation? First, understand that when your child gets upset, he is acting from a place of emotion. The same is true for you. When it all seems too much, declare a time-out so that both of you can cool down and process your emotions. Then say something like this to your child: "The way we are doing this isn't working for either of us. We need to start over. We need to find a different way. Let's each think about what that might be."

If you are struggling to find a way to stop a recurring problem with your child, follow this tip: Instead of treating the situation as your responsibility alone to solve, treat it as a mutual concern. Enlist the child's ideas to help solve the problem. Two heads are often better than one.

BUILDING BLOCKS OF COOPERATION

At around age three to four, your child should begin learning the basics of cooperation. This, like any other skill, can be taught through repetition. Because repetition builds habits, focusing on cooperation early will help you to encourage a healthy partnership between yourself and your child.

○ **Listening and attending:** "What did you hear me ask? Please tell me what I just said." You want your child to be in the habit of tuning you in, not tuning you out. Your child thinks, "I know what you want when I pay attention to what you say." Likewise, model by repeating what your child has said to you, along with your interpretation. "I heard you say that it's hard for you to finish your homework like I asked you to, because you're having a hard time concentrating while you can hear your sister playing outside."

○ **Giving to get:** "What do I need you to do for me? Tell me what you do for me that gets me to do for you." Providing a clear description will help your child to learn this concept. Start by telling her "I need you to sit in your seat before I give you your teddy bear." To clarify, you might say "Tell me what I want you to do, before I give you your teddy bear." You want your child to be in the habit of thinking about how his meeting your needs is connected with you meeting his needs. He thinks, "I do *this* for you and you will do *that* for me."

○ **Keeping agreements:** "What did you promise me? Tell me what you agreed to do." You want your child to be in the habit of keeping his word, not forgetting or breaking it. He thinks, "When I tell you I'm going to do something, I mean what I say." This requires consistency on your part to set an example. Unless you do your best to follow through every time, your child has no framework on which to establish this behavior.

○ **Being of service:** "What special help can you provide? Tell me how I can call on you when I need to." You want your child to be in the habit of valuing what he has to contribute to the family. He thinks, "I have skills worth offering."

Children who are taught early to listen, to give in order to get, to keep agreements, and to be of service to their family—and who are rewarded with praise each time they do these things—tend to be more cooperative with their parents than children who lack these basic interpersonal skills.

Handling Attention Problems

Some children develop a style of relating with others that relies on negative attention. In the absence of any attention, negative attention will do. This "attention-getting" behavior can be trying for everyone involved.

Such children are constantly corrected and frequently punished by frustrated and angry adults, and they often internalize this negative treatment by viewing themselves in negative terms. "I'm bad." "I'm stupid." "I'm a troublemaker." "I'm a loser." They see that adults view them like this, and they come to view themselves the same way. Such name-calling is used to justify treating themselves badly and only lowers their self-esteem.

Although it may take some time and effort, you can reshape a child's behavior. Concentrate on catching your child doing what you'd like her to do, and give her some positive attention—hugging, smiling, or gently tousling her hair. Ignore the bad behavior, unless someone is endangered by it. Minimize nagging and talking too much, as undoubtedly the child has long since stopped seriously listening to adults. Reform the situation according to the old adage "Actions speak louder than words."

GROWING UP IN AN OVERSTIMULATING WORLD

Consider the world of experience and play in which today's children grow up. For many parents, it seems different from the one they grew up in.

- Children are given more information about life and the larger world at a younger age than ever before.

- Children are growing up in a world with an ever-increasing rate of social, cultural, and technological change.

- Children's entertainment is increasingly sensational, violent, and quickly moving to excite interest and appeal to a short attention span.

- Children are given more consumer choices than they know how to make.

- Children are enrolled in more afterschool activities than most of their parents ever were.

- Children have access to more electronic forms of entertainment that require changing attention quickly and multitasking.

- Children are given more toys and possessions than they can use.

- Children are becoming increasingly dependent on external sources of entertainment to escape boredom, becoming less able to entertain themselves.

STIMULATION OVERLOAD

Given all the stimulation from information, entertainment, and the sheer number of choices that children are given today, is it any wonder that they grow up in a state of stimulation overload? Our society has created a disconnect between how children are conditioned by culture and how they are expected to behave at school—to sit still, to be quiet, to follow directions, to focus on one thing at a time, and to spend sustained time working on unexciting instructional tasks.

Discipline Through Medication

In response to a growing population of children who are often inattentive, easily distracted, extremely impulsive, or constantly on the move, parents and teachers may wonder if medication should be considered.

WHY MEDICATE?

Ideally, medication should be given only after a host of other therapeutic and self-management strategies have been given a fair try. Medication—usually psychostimulants—can in some cases slow impulsiveness and the tendency to be distracted, and also increase the child's ability to follow directions and remain focused on a single task.

Just because psychoactive medication has reduced problematic behaviors doesn't mean you should stop teaching your child how to control his impulses and pay attention. Use the break from problem symptoms to continue to teach your child how to develop more physical and social self-discipline.

On the positive side, many medicated children report an improved ability to control impulse, comply with directions, and concentrate on tasks, which results in fewer cases of getting in trouble, and thus fewer blows to their self-esteem.

To medicate or not to medicate your overactive or inattentive child may be the question you face as a parent. Research is ongoing and the choice should always be discussed with your child's doctor. Feeling guilty about placing your child on medication is not healthy for you, or your child. Likewise, you should never consider medication because you feel pressured by others to do so.

TRY TRAINING BEFORE MEDICATION

A good starting point for dealing with attention-challenged children without medication is through occupational or behavioral therapy. Children are taught individual self-regulation skills. With this help, your child can learn to focus on a task, follow directions, and manage hyperactivity. As a parent, you can learn strategies to use at home for reducing distractions, for channeling restless energy, and for using structure, routine, proximity, and touch to help your child focus better and settle down.

Parents have a substantial amount of influence over their children, but they do not, and should not, have control over them. Teaching your children to cooperate with you, instead of struggling against you, will help you raise children who appreciate your values and follow your rules.

Behavior Snapshot

Parenting is a complex job. You as a parent have influence, but are not solely responsible for every aspect of your child's personality. Even children who are consistently exposed to good behavior can resort to using negative behavior to gain attention. Though you may feel that this is an outcome of your parenting and that you are being judged as a result, this is not necessarily the case. Here's a quick scenario that demonstrates how to correctly handle a situation when you feel that others consider you a bad parent.

What happens: At the local farmers' market your toddler is having fun playing with a group of people who have a large container of bubble solution and interesting gadgets to make bubbles of all sizes and shapes. It's time for your family to go and your child begins screaming. Everyone within a twenty-yard radius turns around to stare.

What you *want* to do: Give in to the tantrum and let her stay just to stop the screaming, or give her bottom a smack to show her how bad her behavior is, while demonstrating to those around you that you are being proactive.

What you should do: Firmly hold her against you while she has her tantrum, ignoring everyone looking at you. Remove her from the scene, if possible, perhaps by walking down a side street, and talk to her in a soothing way.

Important Points to Consider

As a parent, not every situation is under your control. Here are some important points to consider:

- In order to change your child's behavior, you may have to change your own.

- There is a difference between parental influence and parental control. We influence by modeling and guiding; we control by force.

- Negative cycles are easy to form and can be tough to break. By looking at the situation as a whole and working as a partner with your child to solve the problem, a negative pattern can be replaced with a positive one.

- There are multiple ways to address behavior and attention problems. When deciding how best to handle an issue, you should not rely on outside pressures or a desire for perfection.

CHAPTER 5

The Principle of Consent

You now know that parents can't control a child's decisions, so how can they guide their children's behavior? The answer is a form of cooperation, and its name is consent. Consent is your child's willingness to go along with what you want and don't want to have happen, to heed your instruction, and to accept your correction.

Consciously Working for Consent

As a parent, you are always working for consent, rewarding the child with appreciation and praise when you get it. Even when you have to remind your child ten times before she empties and refills the litter box for the cat she begged you to get and promised to care for, you sincerely thank her for getting the job done. Otherwise, she will likely complain in return, "You never appreciate what I do!" Your child may be right. Most parents do not appreciate the consent they are given.

To encourage cooperation, always reward your child's consent with expressions of appreciation. It can be as simple as a smile or as warm as a bear hug. Do whatever feels right in the moment.

ACKNOWLEDGING CONSENT

For your child's sake and your own, try to keep in mind at all times the larger picture of what consent is. Even an extraordinarily willful child gives some consent. She does some things that her parents want, and avoids some things that she knows her parents don't want her to do. When a child feels that her parents don't value the consent that she does give, she feels unappreciated and unfairly judged.

The lesson is: always recognize and credit the consent that your child gives you. This recognition will help you maintain a healthy perspective on the times when she refuses to give consent. It also encourages your child to continue giving her consent. Acknowledging to your child that you appreciate that she has done what you want her to do makes her feel that it is worth her effort to do so again.

SEEING THE BIG PICTURE

As a parent, you shouldn't become overly preoccupied with problem behaviors. Problems are by definition negative—something the child is doing or not doing that is wrong in the eyes of the parent and needs to be corrected. Unfortunately, by focusing on what is going wrong, parents often lose sight of all that is going right.

> When parents believe that their child is "nothing but a problem," that negative view can also discourage the child. Parents who view a problem behavior as a small part of a larger person who possesses many strengths can then focus on finding a solution.

Consider a parent who complains to a counselor that his child is completely out of control. "She refuses to get off the phone when I ask, no matter how angry I get. I battle with her about this every night. She won't do anything I say! She's totally defiant!"

If the father is correct, and the child is nothing but disobedient, then he is indeed in a lot of trouble. But the father is not right. He has just become fixated on an ongoing problem, allowing that fixation to take over his entire view of his child.

Compromising to Get Consent

Consent is a compromise for parents. Generally, if you hang in there regarding the issue that's causing problems, being steadfast and not over-reacting, your child will eventually understand your point of view.

At times, when your child doesn't give you consent right away, but rather delays doing what you asked him to do, you may, at first, feel frustrated. However, remember that resistance in families is often a double standard. You may believe that it's okay for you but not for your child. Your child may ask you to do something right away and you say, "Not now, later," resisting because you've had a long day, are feeling tired, or are otherwise occupied. Your delay seems reasonable to you.

Your expectation is that your child will give you immediate attention out of respect for your parental authority. And by the same right of authority, when the tables are turned, you believe your delay is justified because of your child's subordinate position in the family. To encourage your child to comply with your requests more quickly, consider your compliance with his requests, even when your first instinct is to delay.

> How you treat your child is a reflection of how you treat yourself. Yell at your child, and you have just treated yourself as a person who yells. Listen to your child's explanation, and you have just treated yourself as an attentive and patient person.

Delay is always dismissive. When a person doesn't respond right away (whether it is the parent or child who is delaying), it says to the other person, "Your request matters more to you than responding to it means to me right now."

Putting off someone's request can cause that person to feel unimportant, unless the delay is accompanied by a commitment. Thus, when you have to delay responding to a request by your child, it is often helpful to say "Not now, but definitely later" and give a specific time when "later" will occur (for example, "after I finish my phone call"). You can use the same strategy when your child wants to delay responding to your requests: "If not right now, then tell me when." Then hold your child to the time agreed. Delaying a response and then never following up is really just a refusal in disguise.

Handling Frustration

Sometimes the reality of having to wait for or work for consent is more than parents can bear. They get overwhelmed, and they may explode at, threaten, or verbally attack their child. In the process, parents often do or say things that they later regret and the child gets hurt and loses some trust in the safety of the relationship. In addition, she also gains a measure of unhealthy influence over the parent. The child ends up in control when she realizes she has the power to provoke her parents into emotional outbursts.

It is normal for parents to feel frustrated knowing a child can choose to consent or not. Confronted with a difficult problem with their child, they may wish that they could control the child's decision-making, which is, they now know, impossible. But when they lose control trying to force control, the child usually ends up in control, and some injury is often done in the process.

> Parents who lose their tempers when their children deliberately delay responding to a request are giving their children the power to provoke. The most effective parents are those who do not take resistance personally, who stick by their demands, and who refuse to get upset no matter how long it takes for their children to give consent.

DESPERATION STATEMENTS

To avoid conflict, parents should monitor their state of mind while communicating. Parents often make statements out of desperation that demonstrate how frustrated they are feeling, which increases the likelihood of an emotional outburst. A few of the more common desperation statements follow.

- **Statement parent makes in frustration:** "I'm going to keep punishing you until your attitude improves!" **Why is it harmful?** If punishment is all you do, a more negative attitude is all you'll get.

- **Statement parent makes in frustration:** "I'm going to keep taking things away until you do what I say!" **Why is it harmful?** Take away everything the child values, and she has nothing left to lose.

- **Statement parent makes in frustration:** "You're nothing but a problem!" **Why is it harmful?** Any problem is only a small part of a larger person, and parents should keep that larger perspective.

- **Statement parent makes in frustration:** "You're driving me crazy!" **Why is it harmful?** Take responsibility for your behavior. You are choosing to drive yourself crazy on behalf of your child's behavior and then blaming your choice on the child.

Some parents actually encourage opposition by fighting it every step of the way. "We've argued with her from day one about not arguing back when we tell her what to do, and now that she's a teenager she argues worse than ever. She won't give up, she won't back down, she won't change her mind, and she has to have the last word." Arguments create a forum for conflict with parents who argue to get their way. Repeated arguing teaches persistence—the child becomes more invested in arguing with every argument she makes. Be careful not to model the very behavior that you don't want your child to demonstrate.

What is the downside of using physical force to control your child? Parents who rule by brute force and intimidation earn contempt for being adult bullies, not respect for being family leaders.

Dealing with Anger Through Mindfulness

There will be times during your parenting experience when your anger will seem to get the best of you. When you find those powerful feelings coming to the forefront, try any of the following:

○ Separate yourself physically from your child, unless he is a toddler. Then go some distance away, but keep him in view.

○ Notice the physical and emotional sensations that you are feeling. Is your heart rate elevated? Are you perspiring? Do you feel the urge to run or hit? Acknowledge these feelings and use them to help identify triggers and determine when you should disengage.

○ Breathe slowly. Accept your anger and allow it to be replaced by calm.

○ If your child is old enough to be alone for a few minutes or if he is with someone else for a while, take some time alone and regroup.

- If erupting anger is a consistent problem, find an anger management program or a counselor who can direct you in the healing of those issues. It is never okay to hit children, no matter what they do.

- Engage in a physical activity that will help you to deal with and release the emotions building up within you.

- Communicate your feelings to friends, your partner, and, when appropriate, your child. It's perfectly normal and acceptable to feel anger. While this feeling should be controlled, having it does not make you a bad person.

The Power of Choice

In a relationship, choice often equals power. The more choices you have, the more tools you have to influence the other person. If you have no choice, then you have no power.

Thus, in the beginning, your infant feels powerless. By comparison, you appear extremely powerful because you have so many choices as an adult to determine what the child can or cannot have and when she can have it, while the child has far fewer choices of ways to influence you.

When infants discover that two behaviors—crying and smiling—are connected with gaining your attention, that begins to empower them with a sense of influence in the relationship. From here forward, your child's growth is a process of gathering more power of choice as she journeys from dependence to the independence of adulthood.

Your final goal as a parent is to work yourself out of a job, at last turning over the decision-making responsibility to your grown child. Until then, you are using your influence to help your child gather that responsibility in appropriate and constructive ways.

WHEN MISBEHAVIOR CONTINUES

In the normal course of your child's growing up, you will experience times when she continuously misbehaves, defying all your disciplinary efforts. For example, you can't seem to get your daughter to stop throwing tantrums when she is denied something she wants. This is hard enough to deal with at home, but consider a tantrum she throws at the supermarket, with other shoppers staring. She screams, and none of your explaining, orders, or pleading gets you anywhere, and finally you let her have the candy you forbade her to have and she quiets down immediately.

Your child got what she wanted—the candy. You got what you wanted—the end of the tantrum. But now your daughter knows that throwing a tantrum will get her what she wants—while you feel that by giving in, you are encouraging this misbehavior to happen again, which is true. Who has the most influence now?

So what is the solution? First, you must realize that you haven't tried everything. You have allowed frustration and discouragement to wear you down. Brainstorm and replenish your supply of possible disciplinary choices. Remember, behavior is a form of communication, so keep the root cause in mind. No parent has ever "tried everything," because there are simply too many choices to try.

One way you can get your child to cooperate with you while still giving her a measure of control is to offer a choice within a choice. Say, "Here is what I want. Here are three ways you can make it happen. You can choose which way."

CHILDREN NEED CHOICES, TOO

Because parents control so many circumstantial choices in a young child's life, a child can sometimes feel as if she has no choices at all. This can lead to resistance and the attempt to regain power by making negative choices.

A resistant child usually needs more choices, not fewer. Even though parents need to keep the choices focused on the well-being of the child, you can offer some wiggle room. For example, you tell the child what help you need, and within prescribed time limits you let her decide when to get the task done. "I would like you to rake the yard. Sometime this weekend before 3:00 P.M. on Sunday is fine with me. The exact time is up to you."

Giving your child a choice makes it easier for her to give you consent. You've showed that you respect her, and not only have you not lost any of your influence as a parent, you've actually increased it.

Internal Locus of Control

Ultimately your aim for raising a child is that he develop an internal motivation for making positive choices. Psychologists call this an *internal locus of control*. This means that the person, regardless of age, does the right thing, even when no one is watching. For example, a school-aged child while walking home picks up some litter and throws it in a garbage can. This is a person who is developing an internal locus of control.

In order for a child to develop such an inner barometer, the parents have to eventually bow out of the picture, trusting that earlier teachings have been effective, so that they can give the child the dignity of being a separate person who has developed an integrated ethic for himself.

Behavior Snapshot

This chapter discussed the issues of choice and frustration and the battles that can erupt over them. Conscious parents give appropriate choices to their children to empower them, acknowledge when their children consent to what is being asked of them, and model the behaviors they'd like to see in their children. Take for example the following scenario:

What happens: Your high school senior wants to stay out all night on Prom Night.

What you *want* to do: Absolutely forbid it. You've heard enough horror stories about all-night partying. She can't go.

What you should do: Compromise. Set guidelines that your teenager will comply with; for example, to call you at agreed-upon times during the night, indicating where she is and that everything is going smoothly. Perhaps extending her curfew for a night is a possibility. Allow her to have a good time, but in a safe way.

Important Points to Consider

Acknowledging your own leadership, while also gaining consent from your child, is an important concept of conscious parenting. Gaining consent is not the same as "giving in." Allowing children to feel as if they have a choice will lead to positive decision-making. There are many ways to encourage consent:

O Each time that a child consents, you should acknowledge your appreciation.

O Pleading or demanding for consent shifts the power in a relationship. Allowing children to make appropriate choices encourages mutual respect.

O Lack of compliance can lead to high frustration levels. It's okay to take a time out and allow yourself to accept your anger and deal with it.

O Providing choices enhances a child's ability to make decisions that are ethical, even when you're not around.

CHAPTER 6

Communicating with Courtesy

Courtesy is not always appreciated when it's given, but always missed when it's not. Courtesy means using small acts of consideration to signify special caring for another person. The concept of courtesy is crucial to discipline for the conscious parent. Even infants and toddlers respond well to true respect and positive speech.

Dignity of Personhood

It helps to remember that an accident of time has placed you in a position of authority. Imagine your child as a peer who happens to be younger and smaller. Speak to him as kindly as you would to any other person of your acquaintance. Remember that courtesy matters.

"You never asked me!" complains the child. These are frustrating words for a parent to hear. But, in many cases, the child is right. Being asked feels much better than being told, because being asked is an act of courtesy. When you're requesting—rather than demanding—cooperation, you demonstrate that you aren't taking the child's cooperation for granted. To the child this courtesy conveys something big—respect.

Small acts of courtesy represent larger values in relationships. To be praised, complimented, thanked, hugged, listened to, and included encourages both you and your child to feel good about your relationship. By the same token, because you are tired from work and your child is tired from school, you may each decide to let these small things go. So you are not thanked for remembering to pick up your child's school supplies, and your child is not listened to when he is describing a painful part of his day. If you don't use courtesy, the neglected person feels wounded by the other person's insensitivity.

When your child has omitted a significant courtesy, don't let it go. Speak up about the slight you feel. Likewise, acknowledge your child's requests for courtesy, spoken or implied.

The Power of Discourtesy

When you are under stress or are preoccupied by problems with your child, you can easily commit acts of discourtesy that lead to damaging effects. Let's imagine that you're having a difficult day—it's raining, you're late, you drop your wallet and the dog snatches it up to play a friendly game of chase. You shout at the dog in anger. Your child says, "You'll scare him if you talk so loud!" You shout at your child, "Who asked you?!" Other instances of discourtesy could be:

O Instead of praise, parents snap at a child.

O Instead of compliments, parents give the child criticism.

O Instead of saying thanks, parents take the child's cooperation for granted.

O Instead of giving hugs, parents give the child no loving touch.

O Instead of being listened to, the child is ignored.

O Instead of being included, the child is excluded.

What's happened to the quality of the child's relationship with her parents now? While absence of courtesy can hurt, acts of discourtesy can cause significant damage to a child's self-esteem. "You treat strangers who come to the door nicer than you treat me! And I'm your child. Aren't I worth treating nice, too?" And then parents wonder why their child has a negative attitude and is resistant to their requests.

How you treat your child teaches that child how to treat you in return. If you want courtesy from your child, then model it.

Teaching Your Child to Apologize

In the give-and-take between parents and child over the normal course of growing up, injury is bound to be given and received by both parties. Someone speaks an impulsive word, breaks an important agreement, tells a lie, forgets a commitment, or otherwise mistreats another family member. A sincere apology is important when either the parent or the child wrongs or hurts the other. Why? Because at issue is developing two important components of discipline: conscience and self-correction. A sincere apology can encourage both you and your child to:

- Recognize the difference between doing right and doing wrong, and subscribe to doing right. Sincere apologizing begins with the honest acknowledgment of how one has mistreated others.

- Own and accept responsibility for giving injury or doing wrong.

- Express sorrow and appropriate guilt after hurting someone through ignorance, accident, or intent. Sincere apologizing is motivated by true remorse. It is possible to express remorse while at the same time accepting that making a mistake is okay.

- Commit seriously to not repeating a wrong or injury that has just occurred. Sincere apologizing carries with it the firm intent to reform.

- Make amends by hearing out the wronged or injured party. Sincere apologizing means that you patiently commit to listening whenever and for however long the hurt person needs.

Remember to praise and reward your child for accepting responsibility. If you do the same yourself, it sets a good example. Teaching a child to appropriately apologize allows him to learn to accept himself, while acknowledging that he's made a mistake.

So how can you teach sincere apologizing? Apologizing must be modeled for it to be learned. Parents who refuse to acknowledge mistakes encourage children to follow that example.

Having a sense of humor can help you from becoming overwhelmed. Laughter helps you step back and see the silliness in your reactions.

Modeling Forgiveness to Let Go of Hurt

Why should you forgive? The first reason the injured party needs to forgive, after receiving a full apology, is to let go of hurt that has been received. Holding on to hurt only nurtures grievance and encourages resentment.

Additionally, forgiving allows the injuring party to let go of guilt. Holding on to guilt only continues self-punishment. When it comes to the philosophy of conscious parenting, forgiveness plays a central role. It is an important release for both the injured and injuring parties. Just as you forgive your child, be prepared to forgive yourself. Modeling this concept for your children will save them future grief caused by holding grudges.

FORGIVENESS AS A SHIFT IN FOCUS

There is a subtle difference between forgiving someone who has done something hurtful to you (exonerating them, rising above it, and trying to take the higher road) and genuinely shifting your focus to other things so that the hurt is no longer a preoccupation. This is a truly healthy type of forgiveness that brings freedom from the original sting.

THE PROBLEM OF NO REMORSE

Should you forgive a child whose actions have been hurtful to you but who expresses no remorse? "Since I didn't mean to hurt you, I have nothing to apologize for. How was I to know my getting into trouble at school would mean you had to leave work to come and get me out?" Should you forgive this unrepentant offender? Yes. But not before trying to help your erring child make some empathetic connection to how you were affected emotionally.

CREATING AN EMPATHETIC CONNECTION

To garner an empathetic connection, first ask the child to reverse roles with you and see what that feels like. "So there you are, in the middle of giving a group book report, and suddenly you have to leave class because you've been called to the principal's office. What are the other people in your group going to think of you for leaving like that? Do you think your teacher would give you a good grade?"

Children can be so preoccupied with satisfying their own needs that they don't consider the effects of their actions on others. Many times they don't intend to offend or injure, but they do. Sincerely apologizing helps the child to become more emotionally sensitive to others. Apologizing is not a skill that we are born with. Children learn the art of apologizing from their parent's example.

If you want courtesy from your child, courtesy must be modeled. When you as a parent commit a wrong, own up to what you did or said, apologize and make amends, resolve not to repeat the offense, and then forgive yourself. Ongoing guilt only erodes effective parenting.

Even after working toward an empathetic connection, there will be times when you still feel hurt by a child who, after listening to your explanation, continues to truly believe she did nothing wrong. "You took away my phone, so I hid yours so you would know how it felt." Should you still forgive if there is no remorse? In certain cases, you should. For your own sake, you should still forgive the child. No good purpose is served by carrying an emotional burden while the young offender lives free of the hurt and anger.

WHEN NOT TO FORGIVE

Are there times that you should not forgive? Yes. If after committing a wrong and apologizing for injury that was done, the child then goes out and repeats the same offense, further forgiveness would only make it easier for the child to continue or repeat the wrong behavior. Thus, in this situation, you declare, "The only sincere apology I will accept is not in your words but in your actions."

Also, there is one category of wrongdoing you should never accept—deliberate acts of wrongdoing committed with malicious intent. Malicious acts of harm are unforgivable and should not be forgotten so they will not be repeated. Just file them away and keep them filed away, as long as they do not occur again. "Threatening violence to your sister to scare her is absolutely wrong! We will not have any member of this family doing, or threatening to do, another family member harm. We will have a safe and fear-free home for every family member."

Communicating the Wrong Message

Parents should beware of confusing their own self-interest with the interests of their child. We live in a competitive society, and that competition can influence your parenting. "How good I am as a parent is measured by how well my child performs and achieves." "The parent whose child does best, wins." Wins what? Social standing among parental friends? Bragging rights? "If my child does better than yours, then I'm a better parent."

Competitive parenting exploits the efforts of children in order to enhance the standing of their parents. Parents, in an effort to satisfy their own ambitions, may subject their children to excessive pressure. "We just want the best for you" can communicate a different message to the child who knows that what it really means is "We want the best from you." A surefire antidote for this unbalanced dynamic is to keep your own life full and rich. Maintain your interests and keep developing as an individual. Cultivate your passions so that you have something to think about and talk about besides the stellar qualities of your children.

> To be a good parent, you don't have to do everything right. Like your children, you will make mistakes. Accepting your own mistakes and imperfections can actually allow you to be a more effective parent.

Adjusting for Growth Cycles

How you communicate best with your child depends partly on how receptive he is to you, which means understanding that there are growth cycles that every child experiences. Understanding these can help make your communication more effective.

It's a phrase you've probably heard to describe a young child at a particularly hard-to-manage age: "He's in his terrible twos." What's so terrible? For parents, the child seems more contrary, more curious, and more committed to following his inclinations. This is a change from the more docile and tractable person he so recently used to be. Now he's insisting on doing what he wants and getting what he wants, and when you get in his way, he lets you know he doesn't appreciate your opposition.

WHAT'S GOING ON?

Every few years (from age two through adolescence), a new growth cycle seems to occur. Your child becomes discontented with the limits of freedom you've established for him. Growth cycles begin with the child breaking the traditional boundaries that circumscribed allowable behavior to create more room to grow. This is the child's job—to push for further growth when he feels ready. Your job is to encourage growth within the limits of safety and responsibility.

For example, your two-year-old (as thrilled by the mobility of walking as your sixteen-year-old is with being able to drive a car) believes he should be able to go wherever he wants, whenever he wants. As parents, you insist on teaching the child to manage this new freedom responsibly. You do not allow him to run anywhere he wants outside, any more than you let the sixteen-year-old drive wherever and whenever she wants.

HOW GROWTH CYCLES WORK

Growth cycles unfold in three phases. The first is *disintegration*. Disintegration begins when the child becomes sufficiently dissatisfied with his current place in life to begin breaking old boundaries of prescribed conduct. It's as if the child is saying to himself, "I am no longer content with the restrictive terms I have been living under."

Growth cycles are a healthy part of development and should be expected to create discipline problems as your child pushes for new terms on which to live, some of which will be acceptable to you and some of which will not.

The next stage—*exploration*—begins when the child, now eager to discover new ways of acting, uses the new freedom he has gained to experiment with different behaviors. At this middle stage of the cycle, the child can become more unpredictable for parents to live with, and they are at risk of becoming anxious in response.

The third stage is *consolidation,* and it begins when the child, now desiring to get his new growth under control, incorporates the new behaviors into a new self-definition. It's as if the child says to himself, "I like what I have gained and what I have become." At this final stage of the cycle, the child becomes more consistent for parents to live with, and parents are at risk of their relief's denying the inevitability of more growth cycles to come.

GROWTH CYCLES AND DISCIPLINE

Each time a growth cycle occurs, your existing disciplinary structure will be tested and often modified. As your child experiences healthy growth, you will change your disciplinary structure in response—less than the child wanted, but more than you had planned. That's the compromise of child raising.

Behavior Snapshot

This chapter discussed the concepts of conscious courtesy and remorse. Everyone gets angry and makes mistakes, and when this happens you need to apologize with sincerity, as does your child. Forgiveness will strengthen the bonds of trust while yelling and harsh punishment only serve to break them. Here is what demonstrates forgiveness:

What happens: Your teenager has borrowed the car, with your permission, and brings it home with a dinged fender.

What you *want* to do: Shout at her in outrage, "That's it! You can't use the car anymore! When are you ever going to learn to take care of other people's property?"

What you should do: Take a deep breath. Listen to her version of what happened. Work out a way for her to pay for the repair—extra jobs for the household, deductions from her allowance, or a temporary part-time job.

Important Points to Consider

Acknowledging the personhood of your child means treating him with the same courtesy that you'd extend to older family members, coworkers, or friends.

O Courtesy is crucial to maintaining a relationship that is built on a foundation of mutual respect.

O Acts of discourtesy can lead to long-term relationship wounds. When modeled, discourtesy encourages your child to treat you without respect.

O Modeling and encouraging your child to offer sincere and appropriate apologies encourages emotional growth and development of empathy.

O As your child begins a new growth cycle, it's important to acknowledge this healthy development and adjust your discipline methods.

 **CHAPTER 7**

Consciously Dealing with Differences

If all children were the same, developing a discipline strategy for the whole family would be a breeze. And if both parents saw eye to eye on everything, they might find it easier to make discipline decisions together. If your children were just like you, you'd know exactly how to handle them. But, of course, this is not the case. Conscious parents embrace diversity.

Recognizing and Respecting Different Personalities

What works with one child may not work well with another. It is this natural human individuality that makes the process of discipline more complex. Some children require intense discussion and effort on your part before they will give their consent and accept discipline. Other children prefer being obedient to taking the time and effort to resist or fight your rules. Some children demand to know your reasons, while others will accept rules without many questions.

One of your first jobs as a parent is getting to know your child. What is her temperament? What sensitivities does she have? What about aptitudes, and what kind of personality does this little person possess? Just because your first child was docile doesn't mean that your second child will be the same way.

The parents of multiple children can still have the same family rules and values for each, but the way they practice discipline should cater to the personality and unique needs of that child.

Discipline does *not* mean treating all your children the same way. Although you may have the same disciplinary code—or values—with all your children, you should vary your disciplinary approach based on each child's temperament and personality traits.

Within the first three or four months of your child's life you should have some sense of her temperament (calm or excitable, for example), sensitivities (comfortable or uncomfortable with touch or noise), aptitudes (quickly or gradually responsive to visual or spoken cues), and personality (quiet or sociable).

In addition to having different personalities from one another, your children also have different personalities from you. It is easier for parents to understand and relate to a child who is, by nature, similar to them than to relate to a child with different personality traits.

For the sake of your personal comfort, you might feel like trying to change the child's temperament to suit your own. "I've got to get her to slow up and quiet down." Inborn traits are not easily changed, and your efforts to change them may feel like a form of rejection to your child. The risk is that the child may begin to believe "There must be something the matter with me because I am not exactly like my parent. I am not okay the way I am."

Two Parents, Two Views

All families have systems of beliefs, with no two families sharing all the same rules and values. Each family also has its own disciplinary code. In two-parent families, that code is a combination of rules and beliefs that each parent deems important. And since each parent comes from a separate and distinct family background with different childhood experiences, all parenting partnerships are to some degree cross-cultural. This means that putting together a unified disciplinary approach will require understanding, accepting, and bridging the traditional differences that each brings to the table.

Having different values from your spouse regarding parenting is common. Treat differences not as a source of divisiveness, but as a source of richness and strength. Two of you are wiser than one because your two points of view offer a broader vision than a single one.

RESOLVING VALUE CONFLICTS

So what should you do when a conflict over disciplinary values arises? First, respect your partner's values. "We judge this situation differently, and that's okay." Second, specify each person's "wants." You want to pick up the infant right away. Your spouse wants to let the child learn to tolerate some mild discomfort. Third, without challenging or criticizing the value differences, negotiate a compromise of wants. So you agree on a time limit, after which if the fussing continues, you will go in and pick up the infant.

Value differences between parents over discipline, how to instruct, and how to correct will continue over the course of your parenting.

You don't have to convince your spouse that the reasons behind your values are valid. You just have to reach an agreeable compromise.

Part of your commitment to each other as parents is to communicate for however long it takes to reach a disciplinary decision you can both live with and support. Part of your authority as parents is demonstrated by displaying a united front that cannot be divided and exploited by a manipulative child. The main rule to remember is to never let parenting differences or decisions over discipline become divisive to the partnership.

Balancing Acceptance and Demands

Because love is based on acceptance, and training (where discipline occurs) is based on making demands, parents often vary in which of these two parenting components they are most comfortable providing. You may find it easier to provide acceptance, which is appreciated by your child, than to make demands, which often are not. Or you may find it easier making demands than accepting changes that are part of your child's normal growing up.

If you tend to be a highly accepting parent, you may have to work to develop your demanding side—setting limits, stating requirements, and confronting hard issues. If you tend to be a highly demanding parent, you may have to work to develop your accepting side—listening, compromising, and tolerating differences.

If one parent, in an effort to avoid conflict, tends to give most of the acceptance and the other parent, in an effort to control, tends to make most of the demands, this difference can create a divide in the marriage. "You never show love to the kids; all you do is order them around!" "Well, you never get after the kids to behave; you leave all the hard parenting to me!" Whether you're raising children alone or with a partner, you need to have both accepting and demanding sides of your parenting in working order.

Different Genders

Being the only woman in a household of men (when you have only sons), or the only man in a household of women (when you have only daughters), can also cause tension as you try to make equitable decisions about discipline. In this kind of family system, you may feel like a minority within the household because of a strong gender-based culture in the family.

You may hear things like "How can a mother understand her son's needs as a man? As his father, I know best." You might feel like an outsider, excluded from the loop of information in which everyone else is often included. Or a daughter confides to her mother, "I'll tell you, if you promise not to tell Dad—he wouldn't understand." As you lose credibility with your children for being of a different gender, you are told less; as you are told less, you lose credibility for knowing less. In the end these behaviors can marginalize your importance in the family. It is important to keep the dialog open in your family and to continually reinforce to your children that parenting is a partnership and therefore major decisions are made as a team. Discuss any concerns that you might have with your spouse and point it out when you feel isolated because of your gender.

Don't let your worth as a person and parent be diminished because you are a gender minority of one. You will lose self-esteem, your spouse will lose an equal partner, and your children will lose the benefit of your full influence and participation in their lives.

It's okay to respect and appreciate differences that occur naturally due to your child's gender. A child's gender should not, however, be used as an excuse to treat him or her with more or less respect than you would treat any of your other children.

Learning Styles

As you get to know your children, you will also begin to notice their different learning styles. Adults vary in the same way. Consider your own preferred learning styles. Do you learn better when a task is explained verbally, or when it is written down? Do you learn by the action of doing something? Strive to discover the preferred learning styles of your children. One may prefer that you carefully explain something with words (auditory learning), another might prefer a visual chart with symbols (visual learning), and another might require that you take him through the physical motions involved in learning a task (kinesthetic). A child may strongly favor one style or prefer some combination of the three. These distinctions are helpful when deciding how to communicate rules and preferences to your children.

When promoting positive behavior, it is beneficial to consider your child's learning style. If you've asked your child continuously to clean out her closet, with no results, consider her learning style. Is she a visual learner? If so, is giving her verbal instructions going to yield results? Try going together to her closet and collaborating on a to-do list that outlines the basic steps that she needs to take to get the job done. For younger children, pictures could be drawn or printed. Experiment with ways to incorporate your child's learning style into your requests. Sometimes noncompliance is less about willfulness and more about miscommunication.

The Danger of "Good" and "Bad"

Sometimes in families with multiple children, one child will seem naturally similar in nature to her parents and be comfortably inclined to live up to their expectations. To this "easy" child, parents give a lot of approval and very little correction because very little is needed. Another child, however, is determined not to be a clone of child number one, and is perhaps vested with a more stubborn and independent nature. Because of this, he fails to meet certain parental expectations, rejects some of their values, and opposes a lot of their wants. Parents give more disapproval and correction to this "difficult" child.

Over time, parents find themselves modifying their labels for the children, the easy child now perceived as usually "good" and getting more positive attention for being a pleasure, and the more difficult child now often seen as "bad" and getting more negative attention for being a troublemaker.

Although the parents don't always use the words "good" and "bad," the terms are sometimes used by the children themselves, who can then develop an envious relationship with each other. "You're so good, you get all their appreciation and I get none!" "Well, you're so bad, you get much more of their attention than I ever do!" So the good child becomes a magnet for compliments and rewards, and the bad child becomes a lightning rod for conflict and punishment. And the more fully each occupies his or her respective role, the more strongly each feels prohibited from trying each other's role.

Every child needs permission to express his or her unique personhood. To the child in danger of going all "good," declare, "You know, if you do something we don't like or disagree with, that doesn't mean you're bad or that we'll love you any less. It just means you're human like everybody else, like us, sometimes acting to other people's liking and sometimes not." And to the child in danger of going all "bad," declare, "You know, there is much more about you that we love and value than that we disapprove of. Just because we fight a lot over differences doesn't mean all you do is get into trouble. We believe the good in you far outweighs any trouble you might sometimes get into."

Differences between parents (who give discipline differently) and diversity among children (who receive discipline differently) can make it challenging to provide the necessary correction and instruction. The trick is to accept and work with the inevitable human differences that exist in every family.

Behavior Snapshot

Every child is different and deals with unique emotional challenges. Even children within the same family can be polar opposites. You as a parent can still have the same rules and restrictions for all of your children, but to be a truly effective parent to each of them you may have to alter your disciplinary approach based on each child's temperament and personality traits. To get the best out of your children, you should embrace who they are as individuals and not try to force them into being a model of their siblings; otherwise you will foster poor self-esteem and get children who always feel second-rate. For example:

What happens: Your youngest daughter is obsessed with sharks. She spends all her free time reading about sharks and drawing sharks, and begs you to go to the science museum again when you have already been several times.

What you *want* to do: Persuade her to be more feminine. "Why can't you be more like your sister and study ballet and painting?" "We're tired of hearing about sharks!"

What you should do: Encourage her to develop her true interest to the extent that she prefers, as long as her schoolwork is getting done and she does her share of chores around the house. She may turn out to be a gifted marine biologist.

Important Points to Consider

Each and every child is different and, though rules and values remain the same, discipline strategies must often be altered. Accepting your child's unique nature will not only strengthen your relationship, it will also allow you to provide more effective discipline.

- Though two children have the same parents, they are still unique individuals.

- Just as children are different from each other, they are also different from you. Some children identify more with one parent than another, but this does not mean that you should take a primary or secondary role in the parenting process.

O Accepting your child and his unique nature will allow you to build a strong relationship. Comparing or making demands designed to force a child to conform to your ideal will only damage your bond.

O Comparing one child to another is an easy habit to fall into. Accepting each child for who he or she is and encouraging each to be tolerant of the other's uniqueness will allow them to develop a healthy sense of self-worth.

 **CHAPTER 8**

Mindful Parental Authority

Without respect for your authority, your child is not likely to give consent to what you want. While his respect for your authority can be based on love, it can also be based on fear. How you command authority with your child is up to you. Using conscious parenting techniques, you find the path that works best for you and your child. Sometimes this process can take some trial and error, but it is absolutely worth the time in the long run.

Modeling Behavior for Your Child

You are the most important teacher your child will ever have. You get to set the mold for his adult behavior through the choices you make as a parent when he is a child. You don't have to be perfect, but do the best you can to be honorable, and discipline issues will somewhat fall into place.

Choosing to follow a fear-based authority can be costly to your relationship. Children learn to use distance, distrust, and deception as strategies to keep scary authority at bay. If you want a close and trusting relationship with your children as they grow, do not resort to threat, force, or intimidation to get your disciplinary way. Instead, create a safe, loving relationship that your child can truly respect.

A family is not a democracy with elected leaders, where each family member has an equal vote. A family is a loving autocracy, where those with caretaking responsibility—the parents—are in charge of consciously governing those who are dependent on their direction and support—the children.

On the other hand, a parent who just wants to be her children's friend, or who feels insecure or uncomfortable assuming authority, could very easily end up being exploited by the children when they realize how much power they have in the family. In this situation, the children now set the behavioral agenda in the family by dictating wants or threatening upset if their wants are denied. The parent tries to please, tiptoeing around unpopular issues, not wanting to upset the children, indulging them to avoid conflict, placating them to keep the peace. This is not a healthy way to go about instilling values and proper behavior in your children.

Being Deliberate in Your Choices

Conscious parenting requires an intentional, deliberate approach. Establishing authority, though necessary, should be done with care.

Children who grow up in households with harsh parental authority generally end up as adults who either avoid conflict or inflict similar suffering on their own children.

While children being raised by conscious parents do, indeed, grow up in a democratic household, parents are, and should be, the leaders of their households. Establishing structure is one way to create parental authority.

Parents should assume authority within the family unit. Without parents assuming and exercising governing authority, there is no family structure of rules to limit freedom and to prescribe responsibility that children can depend on to grow safely.

Acting deliberately involves understanding the reasoning for establishing a certain parameter, such as parental authority. You understand that without a positive model, a child has no basis on which to structure her life, so a certain measure of authority is necessary to raise a child who shares your ideals and values.

POSITIVE PARENTAL AUTHORITY

Authority is about more than correction. Another side of authority is contributive. As a parent, you exercise contributive authority by providing positives in your child's life that you control—resources, permissions, encouragement, structure, support, advocacy, protection, knowledge, instruction, coaching, and praise, for example. Generally speaking, the more you have to correct, the more you should also demonstrate the positive, contributive side of your authority. Otherwise, your child will begin to feel that your authority is all negative, when it is not.

Yes, you can regain authority once it has been lost. Make a commitment to rewarding the positive behavior your child exhibits and enforcing consequences for her bad behavior.

Talking the Talk and Walking the Walk (Being a Mentor)

Children will absorb more of what you do than what you say. If there is conflict within you, more often than not your children will pick up on this. Following through with physical actions is much more powerful than another lecture. Remember the Charlie Brown cartoons with the teacher portrayed as a constantly squawking voice that says nothing? There is a basis of truth here. For example, you have firmly asked your child to turn off the television after a certain program was finished. He imagines you don't notice that the hour is up and continues to watch another program. You firmly take the remote control in hand, turn off the TV, and place the remote out of reach. No comment.

Authority styles vary from person to person and family to family. Your child's personality and temperament should also be considered when developing your authority style. How you position your authority—whether approachable or absolute—can make a big difference in your relationship with your child.

WHAT'S THE DIFFERENCE?

For the approachable authority, all rules are open for discussion, reasons or values behind them available for examination, arguments to the contrary listened to, and all questions answered, with the understanding that, like it or not, the parent still has the final say.

For the absolute authority, the child's speaking up may be considered "talking back," complaining considered "criticizing," questioning considered "disrespect," and arguing considered "defiance." Absolute authority believes the child should have no say.

By allowing the child to comment on and disagree with disciplinary decisions, approachable authority encourages active, independent thinking: "I speak up when I don't think my parents are being fair."

PROBLEMS WITH ABSOLUTE AUTHORITY

Absolute authority shuts down discussion and dissent, encouraging instead a passive and automatic obedience: "I do whatever my parents tell me, no questions asked." One risk of being socialized to absolute authority in the home is that children may learn that they should follow social directives from any outside authority without question. For example, they may do what a stranger tells them to do, even if it feels wrong, because that stranger is an adult. Absolute parent authorities can encourage children to shut up, give in, go along, and not think about the merits of what is being demanded of them.

Most parents alternate between absolute and approachable authority, depending on the situation. For example, stressed by demand, pressed by time, or faced with an emergency, they may decide that being absolute in their authority is more appropriate than being approachable.

In general, approachable authority has less of a downside than absolute authority, particularly once the child enters adolescence and has become more resistant to being managed by his parents. Then, approachable authority can offer a compromise that often works well: the child gets to have his say, but the parents get to have their way. Giving your child a chance to voice objections allows him to feel that he's standing up for himself, even though he ultimately consents to what you want him to do. "Okay, I'll help wash the car before going over to my friend's."

Ways You Communicate Authority

No matter how you choose to exercise your parental authority, how you communicate the intent of your authority also makes a difference. You can use concern-based communication or control-based communication.

CONCERN- VERSUS CONTROL-BASED COMMUNICATION

Concern-based communication makes it clear that the parent is focused primarily on the child's welfare and well-being. You are saying,

"Concern for you is my motivation. I don't want you to go to this event because of the risks involved. I'll tell you what they are as I see them. We can discuss them if you want. As your parent, I don't want to send you into a situation with a high likelihood of your getting hurt." You focus on expressing how much you care for the child's well-being.

Control-based communication suggests, however, that the parent is focused primarily on regulating the child's life. You are saying, "Control over you is my motivation. I'll tell you what you can or cannot do. I've decided you can't go to this event. There will be no discussion. You will do what I say. I will get my way."

WHY SHOWING CONCERN WORKS

In general, children often respond better to authority that originates out of genuine concern for the child than control for the adult. Perhaps this is because the concern-based parent seems to be more on the children's side, compared to the control-based parent, who seems to be against them. Concern-based communication also allows children to engage in a dialogue with parents over the issue of disagreement or the problem to be solved. Children understand that parents are respecting their ideas, showing interest in what they have to say, even working out a solution or resolution that benefits from ideas the children have to offer.

Behavior Snapshot

Being an authority figure is part of being a parent. Your children need authority to grow up into successful and happy adults, but some authority styles can lead to conflict. For example:

What happens: Your fifteen-year-old daughter has confided in you that her boyfriend is pressuring her to have sex in order to "prove her love."

What you *want* to do: Send your daughter to a convent and the boy in question to jail.

What you should do: Assure your daughter that you will back her up in every way possible. You can suggest she say that her parents will no longer let her go out with him unless it is a group situation. Keep the channels open and let her know that your cell phone is always on when she is on a date. You will come and get her at any location at any time of the night in order to keep her safe.

Important Points to Consider

Being a conscious parent requires establishing authority, but doing so deliberately. Being a dictator, rather than a leader, will only breed resentment in your parent-child relationships.

- Modeling your values and ideals is one important step toward gaining the respect of your child.

- Authority can be established in an intentional way. By establishing the structure by which you can share your values, you are creating authority.

- How you choose to communicate your authority will determine how well it is received.

 **CHAPTER 9**

Raising Responsible Children

If you had to choose only one goal of discipline, raising responsible children would be a good option. When you teach your child what constitutes responsible behavior, you implant a code of values she can follow for the rest of her life that will favor doing what is right over doing what is wrong. When you teach your child responsibility, you are giving her the mechanism to learn from experience. This is an important skill that your child will carry with her throughout the rest of her life.

Two Elements

If a responsible child is one who has been taught responsible behavior and responsibility, how are you going to help your child develop both of these attributes? To begin with, you need to be very clear about the difference between the two concepts. They are not the same.

RESPONSIBLE BEHAVIOR VERSUS RESPONSIBILITY

Responsible behavior is the governing of one's conduct according to ethical standards one has learned: "My parents taught me that being thrifty means not wasting what I use." *Responsibility* is the capacity to own the consequences of one's decisions: "I got a speeding ticket because I wasn't watching how fast I was driving."

Teach responsible behavior by limiting freedom and prescribing choice. "To save electricity, turn off the lights when you leave a room." Teach responsibility by giving freedom and permitting choice. "How you drive is now up to you, as is coping with the consequences of whatever driving choices you make." Parents teach responsible behavior by holding on, and teach responsibility by letting go.

WHY LEARNING BOTH MATTERS

One shouldn't automatically assume that because a child has learned one concept she has also learned the other. For example, a well-behaved child is not necessarily a child who has learned responsibility. Raised in strict obedience to stern parental authority "or else," a child may have learned the rules of responsible conduct that her parents taught her, but she has never been given sufficient freedom of choice to learn to own the consequences of independent choice, having always done only what she was told to do.

Practice socially inclusive parenting. Don't send children away when adult company arrives or seat them at separate tables when it's time to eat. Instead, let them join in conversation with grown-ups and they will develop translatable social skills.

Consider a child who has learned the enormous power of responsibility, but may never have been taught any rules for responsible behavior. Neglected by parents too preoccupied to care, the child is given great freedom to learn from natural consequences of choices made but is uninstructed about what constitutes responsible behavior.

Teaching Responsible Behavior

Every family defines what constitutes responsible behavior differently, depending on the values the parents hold. However, it is taught the same way in every family—by example and instruction.

TEACHING BY MODELING

With a child too young to be instructed verbally, you must demonstrate how you want things done by using yourself as an example. Consider teaching a two-year-old "responsible" eating behavior. You want him to learn to use a spoon, not just his hands. So, as much as possible, you make it an imitation game. First, you put the spoon of food in your mouth and smile. Then the little child attempts to do the same and laughs with delight as this game of imitation builds between you. As the repetition continues, your child learns something serious from play. Reward desirable behavior with a smile and a cheer when it occurs.

> Though parents often begin by using mostly positive responses to shape a young child's behavior, they typically resort to more negative responses as the child grows older. Rewarding the positive is more effective than punishing the negative, no matter what the child's age.

Hygiene, picking up, cleaning up, and putting back are all taught in the same way. By keeping instruction light and playful, you make it a game.

And you use very little negative correction, and then only of the most gentle kind.

When the child hits you in the face because he feels angry for being put to bed, clasp the child's hands, look him in the eyes, and seriously (not angrily) repeat the word "No" while shaking your head. Then you hug him and smile and put him down. If he hits you again in anger, repeat the corrective process because, as an adult, you understand that children do not learn from just one episode of instruction. Over time he will come to understand that the headshake "No" means that you don't want him to repeat what he just did. Obviously, you do not want to hit a child for hitting, or yell at a child to stop yelling, because that only teaches by example the behavior you wish to stop.

A Model for Teaching Responsible Behavior

One way for parents to structure their instruction of responsible behavior is around the concept of care. Develop a curriculum that you want to teach. Here is a framework of suggested topics.

- **Caring for self:** maintaining one's own health and hygiene, care of space and possessions, cleaning up and picking up after oneself, providing for and protecting oneself.

- **Caring for family members:** showing consideration, sharing what one has, helping others out, providing support during difficult times.

- **Caring for the family unit:** contributing to chores and services, compromising for the larger good, communicating about common concerns.

- **Caring for others:** respecting rights of others, obeying social rules, showing concern for human welfare, volunteering community help.

Establishing categories of responsible behavior is the first step in your discipline process. The second is specifying the actions that will put those behaviors into actual operation. The third is having the child repeat these actions often enough so that responsible behavior becomes a habit. When it comes to caring for others, it will seem only natural to your child, after having practiced this on a regular basis in the family, to spend some volunteer time each month helping others less fortunate than herself.

> One way to reinforce the importance of responsible behaviors is to get your child involved with other people—good friends, extended family, or place of worship, for example—who practice your values of responsible conduct.

A final way you teach your child responsible behavior is to depend on her to help fulfill family needs. The message is "To function as a family we need your participation, contribution, and help." This will engage your child and help her understand that she is an important part of the family.

Teaching Responsibility

Responsibility is one of the most difficult skills for parents to teach. The decisions about when to let go and what choices to turn over to the child can be complicated.

Let go too early and the child may be at risk of immature judgment. For example, excited and overconfident from learning to balance on a bike, believing that that is all there is to riding, the child takes off down the street, gathers speed, and crashes into a parked car because steering is not yet under control.

Let go too late and your child might be at risk of inexperienced decision-making. For example, by waiting until the late adolescent is older before teaching him how to manage his credit, he blithely overcharges a credit card in college and gets into serious debt.

Since responsibility requires taking risks as your child tries to handle a new freedom on his own, first determine what kind of risk-taker your child is—very bold or very cautious. You may have to restrain the bold child with caution and embolden the cautious child with encouragement.

TURNING OVER RESPONSIBILITY

Teaching responsibility in an appropriate fashion is labor intensive. The following is a list of tips to help you during this process:

1. You show the child how to do something by explanation and demonstration.

2. You help the child to do it with your advice and support.

3. You monitor how the child does it with supervision.

4. You let the child practice it on his own within limits suitable for a beginner.

5. You turn over responsibility by letting go, letting the child do it independently.

6. You hold the child accountable for good and bad consequences, reviewing the lessons that both kinds of consequences have to teach.

SEPARATING RESPONSIBILITY AS CHILDHOOD ENDS

A child usually enters early adolescence somewhere between the ages of nine and thirteen as he becomes more discontented with being defined and treated as a "child." Participating in older-age activities and experiencing the larger world outside of family now become more important as the young person begins to push against, and pull away from, parents for more freedom to grow.

From this critical growth point onward, the great protector for the child is going to be the power of responsibility he possesses to make mindful and unimpulsive decisions as he experiments with new and different experiences. To safeguard a child's early adolescence, parents need to begin turning over three kinds of self-management responsibilities—facing consequences of bad decisions, recovering from unhappiness, and solving problems.

So rather than rescue the child from the consequences of a bad decision, parents should help the early adolescent to take more responsibility for dealing with the outcomes of his actions. "We think you need to pay for what you did." Rather than provide some fix for the child's unhappiness, parents should enable the early adolescent to take more responsibility for recovering his own emotional well-being. "We want you to develop ways to cheer yourself back up when you are feeling down." Rather than jumping in and solving the child's problems, parents should encourage the early adolescent to take more responsibility for figuring out his own problems. "We want you to think out some possible solutions before we add any of our own."

Teaching Two-Step Thinking

One approach to teaching your child responsibility is through a process where you help her develop the habit of thinking twice. This means helping your child learn the discipline of two-step thinking.

Consider this: When an infant is born into your care, she is a one-step or first-step thinker. What is this first step? It is the infant's knowing what she wants. Immediate gratification of wants is the infant's ruling impulse. As parents, you appreciate the importance of wants and urgency of impulse, but you know that a life governed only by wants and impulse will become destructive. This is why your job is, through discipline (instruction and correction), to train the growing child, over time, to become a two-step thinker.

What is the second step? The second step of two-step thinking is exercising judgment. You train the child to delay impulsively gratifying wants long enough so she can consider what is wise. You do this by reminding the child to think about consequences. So when you see your child tempted to rush into a risky decision, you say, "Think twice about what you are going to do." And the child is reminded to delay wants long enough to exercise judgment by considering past and possible consequences. "On second thought, maybe I'll wait until tomorrow to decide what to say to my friend about our fight at school today. I'm feeling pretty hurt and angry right now."

The child takes time to think ahead. Her present choice is being determined by predicting possible outcome. As her want (telling the friend off) is influenced by judgment (taking time to cool down before speaking), your child is learning responsibility.

The Choice/Consequence Connection

Life is a chain of choice and consequence. As adults, you know that a lot of what happens to you is a consequence of decisions you make. Children, however, have to learn this connection.

"I want to go outside and play," says the child.

"I want you to be able to go out and play, too," agrees the parent. "But what do you need to do first before you get to go outside?"

"Pick up my clothes," answers the child.

"That's right," congratulates the parent. "You can choose to pick up your clothes so you can get to go outside and play."

Sometimes the choice/consequence connection can be hard to learn because children are, by nature, shortsighted. They focus on what they want now, not considering how choices now can cost them later. So the child spends his three dollars at the corner convenience store this morning on an impulse buy, forgetting that he was going to save it for admission to a movie this afternoon. Why didn't he save his money? Because he was thinking only about the "now," not connecting it with the "later."

WHO'S GOT THE PROBLEM?

As parents, you sometimes must resist the temptation to protect your child from the consequences of his bad decisions. If you constantly intercede between your child's choices and the bad consequences they create, then the problem that was originally your child's will become your own, your child will learn no lesson from the consequences he chose to create, and the same bad choices are more likely to continue.

So parents complain about their first-grader who, despite their reminders, leaves new toys outside overnight. But then, after the child is in bed, the parents go and bring in the toys because they don't want their son to be victimized by theft and to suffer the consequence of loss and disappointment that would follow. Unfortunately, by sparing him this unhappy consequence, they are also keeping him from learning the responsibility that goes with taking care of his toys. One of the most difficult parts of parenting is letting your child face the consequences of his bad choices, learning from whatever hard lessons the choice/consequence connection has to teach.

When parents pay for their child's consequences to protect their son or daughter from hurt, they usually buy the child's problem for themselves at their own and their child's expense.

NATURAL CONSEQUENCES

When a child experiences natural consequences from poor choices that he regrets, parents do not need to add correctional consequences of their own to teach a lesson. Instead, they can support the child with sympathy and explore what the unwanted consequence has to teach. So when your son neglected to bring in his newest toy from the backyard at the end of the day as reminded, he found it missing the next morning. He's crushed and wants to know if you will replace it. No, you tell him, gone is gone. But you can express sympathy that it happened, then ask what he's learned from the loss.

Before applying any negative consequence for their child's misbehavior or mistake, parents need to ask themselves, "Has any natural or other social consequence occurred that will discourage this choice from being made again?" If so, don't pile on additional consequences.

OUTSIDE SOCIAL CONSEQUENCES

In the same way, when a second-grader is given lunchtime detention for a repeated classroom offense, and so misses out on socializing with friends, parents do not need to apply consequences for that classroom misbehavior at home. The school has given a consequence of its own. All you need to do as a parent is help the child see the connection between how he chose to act and how the school chose to respond. "We're sorry you missed lunch with your friends. How can you manage to behave in class so this doesn't happen to you again?"

Casting Off Responsibility

One helpful guideline to follow when teaching your child responsibility is that accidents aren't excuses. Don't let your child attempt to cast off responsibility for her actions by claiming something was an accident. Instead, help her to see how her actions led to that end result.

"It was an accident!" protests the child about how papers in the trash caught fire. "I didn't mean to set a fire. I thought the match was out." Lack of intent does not excuse the child from responsibility. "If you hadn't been lighting matches, there would have been no opportunity for the trash to catch fire." The child may well be innocent of intent, but the child is guilty of unthinking (and, in this case, forbidden) actions leading to an unacceptable outcome. "This is why we have a rule against your playing with matches. To prevent accidents."

The less a child values herself, the less responsibility for mistakes and misbehavior she is likely to accept, because she feels so inadequate already. Children who claim it is never their fault when it actually is are often troubled by low self-esteem.

Another helpful guideline is "no blame allowed." Accepting some degree of responsibility empowers the child with the choice to influence whether whatever happened will happen again. So parents work with the child to figure out if there was anything she could have done differently to have done better.

Counting and Earning Systems

Two time-honored training techniques of parents have been systems of counting (toward consequence) and earning (rewards). Both systems teach the child to connect choice with consequence.

Some parents with a low tolerance for frustration use another age-old counting strategy to keep from losing their temper with a willful child. Counting to ten can help them cool down and maintain self-control to prevent overreaction.

Counting systems tend to be based on avoiding negative consequences. What counting does is put the child on notice about how a choice now will soon lead to an unwanted consequence. Counting gives the child time to think. Does the child really want to pay the consequence for continuing to do what he has been asked to stop? The choice is up to the child, and the parent formally acknowledges that choice. Now the child knows, "I affect what my parent will do based on the choice I make."

It's also important to take the time to consider the reasons for a child's behavior. Behavior is, after all, a form of communication. Counting is one way that you can allow yourself to step back and look at the big picture.

Earning systems are based on gaining positive consequences. "I have posted a list of five things I want you to do every weekday to help me at home. At the end of each week we will check off which ones you have done. For twenty-five checks, you get to pick out a movie to rent. For twenty to twenty-four checks, you get to pick out a favorite meal. For fifteen to nineteen checks, you get to go out for ice cream." The weekend has become reward time for working hard all week.

With earning systems, a child attaches choices made now with gaining something special later. In addition, the posted list of "five things" serves as a daily reminder for the child about what parents want him to regularly do for them. Earning systems work when the rewards being offered are ones that the individual child values, and the rewards earned are promptly and faithfully provided.

Behavior Snapshot

In order for your children to become well-adjusted adults you must teach them both responsibility and responsible behavior. They need to be accountable for the actions they take (responsibility) and choose to make sound decisions based on the ethical values they have been taught (responsible behavior). For example:

What happens: Your gifted middle-schooler has decided after the school year has already begun that she wants to be in the gifted program. You and she had talked about it during the summer, and she opted for the regular track. The reason for her changing her mind? A cute boy in the gifted program.

What you *want* to do: Say that it's already been decided and she has to stick with the plan.

What you should do: Say that you will support her in the change, but she has to make her own arrangements with the school psychologist and counselor for testing and placement in the new group.

Important Points to Consider

Raising responsible children is a complicated and time-consuming process, but it's well worth the rewards.

- O There are two elements to responsibility: responsible behavior and responsibility. A child can demonstrate one skill and not the other.

- O Teaching two-step thinking encourages your child to establish his wants and then exercise good judgment in obtaining them.

- O Allowing your child to experience consequences will encourage him to become a stronger decision-maker.

 **CHAPTER 10**

Guidance: The First Factor

The first factor in effective discipline is guidance. Guidance is largely one-sided communication. It's the parent's asking "What knowledge do I want my child to gain from me?" The purpose of your guidance is to provide information that will help him through the process of growing up. You have the child's best interests at heart because you are connected by love to the child, a claim that other sources of information cannot make.

The Power of Persuasion

For parents who are fearless and respectful communicators, guidance provides most of the disciplinary influence they'll ever need. They do not tiptoe around uncomfortable topics. They are committed to follow through, they do not give up when the talking gets tough, and they are respectful because they listen to, and take seriously, whatever the child has to say, encouraging him to do the same with them.

ADVICE THAT STICKS

Most parental persuasion does not come by way of arguments with your child. It doesn't come from controlling your child's choice of how to think and what to decide. Your ability to persuade comes from influencing your child's choice by offering a piece of advice or a point of view that he is willing to consider. "Just for your information, this is what I think about what you told me and why. And this is what I think is in your best interest."

> When you and your child view an issue differently, you have much more influence when you discuss the issue in order to understand his side, rather than arguing over the issue in order to win.

The role of guidance is to offer an additional value reference to the mix of beliefs created by the child's personal views, the child's peers, and the popular culture he encounters every day. A parent's job is not to change the child's mind, but to offer a responsible alternative frame of reference on an ongoing basis.

For example, peers may be telling your child how funny it is to egg the front door of someone they don't like. As parents, you may disagree. "How you think about this is up to you, but just for the record, I see it a different way. I think when people deliberately deface other people's property, they are doing injury to those people and should have to pay for what they do." Don't argue with the child's opinion, because that will just strengthen the opposition between you. Your input is more powerful than your argument.

"You have a right to your opinion. I just want you to know, I don't see it that way, and the local police feel the same way. If you choose to vandalize, you may have to deal with severe consequences that are out of my control."

Input respects the child's power of choice, and shows him that you respect him, which means he is more apt to listen to and consider what you have to say. Argument creates a power struggle, where winning (or not losing) becomes more important than gaining understanding.

GIVING GOOD INFORMATION

The most effective parents are not controllers; they are informers. Some hallmarks of a good informer are:

O Willingness to offer alternative opinions, while not insisting on being right.

O Willingness to listen openly to opposing opinions, not with your mind shut down because it is already made up.

O Willingness to discuss differing opinions in order to increase mutual understanding, not turning a difference into an argument you feel you have to win.

Parents don't have to have all the answers. Parents don't have to know what to do in every situation. Many times, the best a parent can offer is "I'll help you think the problem through, and maybe together we can come up with a solution or plan that will answer your need."

Ironically, the power of parental persuasion begins by declaring to the child, "What to think and how to act are ultimately up to you." The power of parent as wise counselor is offering, not ordering. Children who have this parental resource are usually very grateful for it. "I can talk to my mom about anything, and I can always trust her to tell me what she honestly thinks."

Partnering with Your Child

As a parent, you are guiding your child along her path in life. You do this partly by being older and more experienced, and you do it partly in consultation with your child, who informs you about the changed realities of growing up today. An important facet to guiding your child is asking questions about her beliefs, opinions, and experiences. In this way you help her forge a life path that is appropriate to *her own* values and viewpoint.

This is how you form a partnership with your child. This partnership is between a generalist and a specialist, trying to combine the understandings of both to serve the growing needs of your daughter.

THE PARENT AS GENERALIST

You are the generalist. Because you have lived longer, have more experience, and have extensive exposure to the larger world, you have some general understandings about life that your child lacks.

THE CHILD AS SPECIALIST

Your child is the specialist. No one understands her self and her social world better than she does. She is familiar with the peer culture in which she lives in ways you will never be. For example, though the music she listens to may sound strident and abrasive to your ears, it inspires her through the emotional trials of growing up and the longing for independence.

If you can't listen and learn from your child's special knowledge, it is unlikely your child will be able to listen and learn from your general understanding. Your persuasive power is partly dependent on your being open to being enlightened by your child.

Guidance is often a brainstorm between you and your child. When it comes to charting a healthy course for your child's life, two heads are better than one. There's a lot your child doesn't know yet, but there's also a lot you don't know. Never forget that the best informant about the realities of your child's world is your child.

Giving Constructive Feedback about Performance

Since your child is constantly performing (doing chores, complying with rules, doing classroom work), you have a role in monitoring his performance and giving a continuing stream of feedback about how he is doing.

A shortcut way to think about guiding your child through a difficult situation is with the letters FLIP. F: Feelings—acknowledge the child's feelings, "I can see you're really mad." L: Limits—explain the rules, "But we aren't allowed to hit." I: Inquire—ask for the child's input, "What else could you do instead when you are mad?" P: Prompt—give suggestions, if the child can't think of any, "You could ask to pound some Play-Doh, or you could go sit in a safe spot."

As you already know, focusing on positive performance is much more productive than becoming preoccupied with the negative. Noticing, and providing positive feedback and praise when your son continues to get up in time for school, once again has remembered to write down all assignments, and keeps doing homework without being asked, supports continuation of behaviors you want your child to practice.

The fact that today the child had a fight with another child in the lunch line over who got there first (and got sent to the office for it) should not be treated as the only indicator of how he is doing at school. It should be discussed, but within the larger context that this was unusual conduct and not the norm. Where is this behavior coming from, and how should you address the core issue?

EVALUATIVE AND DESCRIPTIVE FEEDBACK

After your child has given a speech as part of a holiday PTA program at school, do you give evaluative or descriptive feedback? Evaluative feedback would be something like "Good for you, you did a great job!" From this, the child knows that his parents have been generally pleased for him, but he doesn't know specifically by what. This is why you need to give descriptive feedback as well. "The way you stood up straight, squared your shoulders, talked slowly and clearly and in a loud voice really made what you had to say effective." When your descriptive feedback itemizes specifics, your child not only feels deeply noticed but can also identify some of the behaviors that contributed to doing a "great job."

Sharing about Yourself

Most of what parents have to give their children is information about who and how they are. "In a lot of ways you're like your dad." One reason adopted children seek out their biological parents is to claim important personal history in order to better understand themselves. An essential part of giving guidance is allowing your children to come to know you, their guide. Both your personal history and your current experience with life have much to teach.

The way you treat your child teaches her how to treat herself. Continually criticize your child, and she learns to become self-critical. Constantly value your child, and she learns to become self-valuing.

SHARING PERSONAL HISTORY

Consider how much guidance you can supply by offering up information about your personal past. By sharing bad decisions you made at their age with your children ("I decided school wasn't worth the effort and dropped out"), you can help them learn from your mistakes.

You can also help them learn from good decisions that you made ("I was badly injured playing sports during my freshman year, but I didn't give up. I worked hard to rehabilitate, and in my sophomore year I was able to play again"). In this case, you give them a personal example of determination. There are powerful cautionary and inspiring stories to be told by sharing your unique personal history.

SHARING CURRENT EXPERIENCE

You also can provide guidance by sharing the experiences from your life as it unfolds. Your child has a problem with her temper when she becomes frustrated at school, so you share your own experiences with effectively managing frustration at work. You also share strategies you have developed to keep frustration from exploding into anger. "I've learned to accept that I get frustrated and shrink my frustrations down to size by comparing them to really serious problems that I'm grateful I don't have. And if I feel myself moving toward anger, I've learned to change my mind and think of happy things instead. These techniques work for me. Maybe they could work for you."

CHILDREN LEARN FROM OTHER PEOPLE'S LIVES

Children are vicarious learners. They learn much about life by hearing about the lives of other people. Think of all they learn about life from the lives of friends. Thank goodness they can satisfy a lot of their curiosity about life without having to actually experience it.

Like your child's friends, you, too, are a window on the world if you allow yourself to be. At the dinner table, you ask about your child's day and get only a minimal reply: "It was okay." You wish your child would share more, but further questions only get more minimal replies. No wonder she is not forthcoming. At the age of twelve, your early adolescent finds your questions intrusive. They invade privacy and are emblematic of authority, often resented and resisted on both counts.

Parents who will not disclose information about themselves usually train their child to respond the same way. If you want your child to confide in you, then confide in your child—not for support, but for education.

So what can you do to encourage more open sharing? Talk about what your day was like, what went well and what went badly, how you felt when things went badly, and how you kept yourself going even so. You can't force your child to talk, but by talking about your own day in specific and emotional detail, you are opening up a window on your world through which your child can see more about life, and you are modeling the sharing behavior you would like her to follow.

Behavior Snapshot

As a parent you have the opportunity to serve as a guide for your child. After all, you've lived longer and experienced more, so why not share that wealth of knowledge? For example:

What happened: Your high-schooler, who consistently gets good grades on his own papers, tells you that a friend wants to hire him to write a term paper. She is willing to pay him a hefty sum.

What you *want* to do: Yell at him and insist that the arrangement is most definitely out of the question. How could he even think of such a thing!

What you should do: Talk with him about the pros and cons of the situation. What is the purpose of the paper? Who gains and who loses if he writes it? If he merely wants to earn money, can you brainstorm other avenues with him? Is the friend pressuring him?

Important Points to Consider

Parents have a tremendous opportunity to teach through guidance. By sharing your own experiences and offering positive feedback, you encourage your child to make good decisions. Consider the following:

O Persuasion occurs not by demanding, but rather by sharing.

O You can view yourself as a generalist, with a general knowledge of how the world works. Likewise, your child is a specialist, with specific expertise in what it means to be uniquely her.

O It's perfectly acceptable to share your experiences and imperfections with your child. This provides her with a window through which she can view situations that she's not yet dealt with.

 **CHAPTER 11**

Supervision:
The Second Factor

The second key technique of effective discipline for the conscious parent is supervision. Supervision is made up of two components—keeping after your child and keeping track of your child. Supervision requires equal parts pursuit and surveillance. Supervision is a necessary evil. It means being willing to back up your requests with repetition and being willing to confirm the whereabouts of your child with checking. Pursuit and surveillance, nagging and checking, are honorable work for which you will get no thanks.

Good Parents Never Give Up

Children dislike being kept after because it makes them feel that they can't escape parental demands. "You already told me! You don't have to tell me again! I heard you the first time! Stop repeating what you said!"

Children dislike being kept track of because it limits their freedom and invades their privacy. "I hate how you keep checking up on me to see where I am and what I'm doing! Don't you trust me?"

> Parenting means never giving up supervision, no matter how unpopular and tiring it feels, because to do so would be to give up responsibility and appear to abandon caring.

Though they complain that supervision is irritating and invasive, children can miss it when parents abandon this responsibility, because of what it symbolically represents. Without enough supervision, children may feel that you've given up on them. Your child may think that you are too concerned with other things to have time for her. Supervision is one way to show a child that you care.

The Power of Pursuit

Some children need gentle reminders to stay on task. "I know this is the third time I've asked you to do your chores, and I'll keep asking you until you get them done." Consistently reminding indicates that parents mean business about getting what they asked for. It works. "I finally did the dishes to get my parents off my back. I was tired of being hassled about it."

PURSUIT, NOT PUNISHMENT

Doing homework and doing chores are supervisory issues and should not be subject to punishment for not being done, because they are nonnegotiable. Punishment says, "If you choose not to do your homework, you will be punished." Supervision says, "You have no choice about not doing your homework. You will do it because I will keep after you and after you and after you until you get it done." You don't punish not doing homework. You use supervision to see that homework gets done.

The same is true with chores. Delay will not make these demands go away. Punishment says, "If you don't do your chores, a negative consequence will follow. This is your choice. This is up to you." Supervision says, "You will do your chores, and I will keep after you until they are done."

It's important to remember that noncompliance is not always the result of a child's choice. For example, imagine that your seven-year-old has spent the afternoon playing intensely in his room. You walk in to find it messier than you've ever seen it. How do you feel? Probably overwhelmed. In this case, simply asking your child to clean his room and then walking away probably won't work. You see, cleaning, especially a really messy room, requires the completion of a series of complex steps. If he sits back down on the floor and begins to play, it's probably not because he wants to disappoint you, but rather he doesn't know where to start. Try breaking the job up into smaller pieces and removing distractions. "Please put your model down and put your clothes in the hamper. When you're done with that, make your bed." Here's where the pursuit kicks in. "I've asked you to put your model down and put your clothes in the hamper. I will keep asking until it is done."

YELLING CYCLES

After giving in to aggravation from asking repeated times for one simple act of cooperation, parents may end up yelling to get what they want, using volume to show how serious they are and to "force" compliance. If you resort to yelling on a regular basis, you will create a vicious cycle.

Supervision is too important to get emotional about, because it turns a performance issue (how parents get something done) into an emotional issue (how the child gets parents upset). Supervision works best when it is calm, unwavering, and inescapable.

Both parents and children usually agree that they all hate the yelling—parents for "having" to do it, the child for having to listen to it. Then why do parents do it? They explain, "Unless we yell, we can't get your attention and cooperation. If you'd just do what we asked the first time, we wouldn't have to yell!" Explains the child, "The reason why I wait until you yell is because by then I know you're getting serious."

Parental yelling models voice-raising to get one's way. It empowers the child—he knows he can upset you by delaying. It actually reduces parental influence by causing parents to resort to more emotional intensity than the situation warrants—a simple task or chore needs to be accomplished. In all these ways, yelling is self-defeating.

Be Relentless, but Not Emotional

Supervisory pursuit is most effective when it is unemotional. Therefore, if you find yourself heating up or getting run down in the process of pursuit, take a break for a while, have your partner take up the chase, or simply give yourself time to calm down. Your child needs to know that even though you may be backing off for the moment, you are not giving up for all time.

Prompting works better than nagging. Cheerfully given and helpfully intended, prompting is pursuit with friendly reminders, requiring you to still feel friendly (not frustrated) in the face of protracted delay.

The issue has not gone away. You will be back. But you will be back on your rational terms, not on yelling terms that undermine your influence and empower the child. Keep on keeping on. Your child will get the message and eventually comply with your request. Children who know their parents won't give up tend to practice relatively immediate compliance. Your relentless insistence will wear down the child's stubborn resistance.

Surveillance

You also need to check on the child when she is away from home. If she thinks she can escape your supervision when she's away from you, you let her know that while you appreciate her feelings, it's a parent's job to ensure that his child is safe.

"I hate it when you chase me down," complains the child. "I can't go anywhere without knowing for sure you won't show up."

"That's right," you agree. "I don't much like doing it either, but I expect you to keep our agreements about where you go and when you're coming back. If you don't, then like you say, I'm coming after you. You decide to hang around the playground and not come in when we agreed? Then I'm coming to the playground to bring you home. If that's what it takes for you to know I'm serious, then you can look for me whenever you decide that it's okay to come home later than the time we set."

Surveillance demonstrates to the child that parents are willing to invade the child's world for good behavior's sake. Parents are willing to vote with their actions to show they mean what they say. It doesn't feel too cool to be busted in front of friends by parents who were willing and able to check up on you by tracking you down.

OVERNIGHTS

One common challenge for supervisory surveillance is checking on the child spending the night at a friend's. The early adolescent wants to be able to make her own social engagements and resents parents checking with host parents to see if these arrangements are as okay as they have been told. "You don't have to call her parents and check. I told you it's okay with them if I spend the night. Are you trying to embarrass me?" No, you are trying to make sure adequate adult supervision is in place. After all, you know about the temptations of forbidden freedom in early and mid-adolescence. There can be a lot of temptation for your child to lie about where she's going and then sneak out with her friends to do something that you would not have given permission for. By checking on overnight arrangements, you can prevent two kinds of end runs. A "single end run" is when your child goes to a friend's house overnight and they both sneak out from there. A "double end run" is when two children tell their respective parents that they are each going to spend the night at the other child's house, but instead take off for a night of forbidden adventure.

If your child insists on sneaking out after hours from your own home or running off, you need to create hot pursuit. If you think you know where the child might be hanging out, go after her. If you think a child's friend might know, call that friend and ask to be told (promise not to tell your child how you found out). If you have no idea where the child might be, call the police and report a runaway. In many cases police will be able to find and return the child to you. All these acts of surveillance let the wandering child know that freedom not responsibly earned will be freedom denied.

ELECTRONIC SURVEILLANCE

Many parents take advantage of the technology of cell phones and smart phones, using them to keep watch on their child. In fact, some children will complain, "You only gave me the cell phone to keep up with where I am!" "That's right," reply the parents. "We expect you to keep the cell phone with you at all times partly so you can call us if you have need, and partly so we can check in with you if we have need. Answering our calls whenever we call is one condition for allowing the freedom we give."

PRIVACY ISSUES

What about your child's privacy? While privacy is indeed important, for children privacy is a privilege, not a right. If your child is keeping you honestly and accurately informed, and is conducting her life in a responsible manner, you can reasonably allow privacy because you are being given grounds for trust. But if she is lying to you, breaking agreements, and violating rules, and she's not explaining this behavior to you, then she has forfeited any right to privacy. Now your invasive surveillance into the child's "private" world is justified. How can you help if you don't know what is going on?

So maybe you discover text messages that outline plans for sneaking friends over when you are still at work and your child is supposedly safe at home, alone, after school. "You spied on my texts?" Your child is outraged. So parents explain, "You cannot electronically communicate without leaving electronic tracks that we can trace if we feel you are not telling us all we need to know about what is going on." Never give your child more online phone or (Internet) freedom than you are prepared to supervise. Remember that behind any behavior is a root cause; this means that risky behavior is often a manifestation of underlying issues, such as low confidence or even boredom.

If your child's life seems to take an inexplicable downward turn into trouble, you might want to start checking where your child goes on the Internet, and checking her e-mail, site visitation, instant messaging, and chat room activity to see to whom and about what your child is communicating. If you lack the technological expertise to do this yourself, get a more computer-knowledgeable friend to help you, or even pay someone who has these digital tracking skills.

TRUST IS EARNED

Your child complains that the constant checking on her feels like mistrust. Explain that trust is earned. When you are absolutely confident that she is trustworthy, you will stop checking. Give some examples in your life along with some examples she can follow in order to earn your trust. Your employer trusts that you will appear for work every day. Your partner expects that you will continue in the relationship in a loving, cooperative manner. Your landlord or mortgage holder expects that you will pay for your housing. These examples will help the child see that trust is an important part of life.

Mutual trust is an important component of a positive relationship. Therefore, giving and gaining trust is an important topic of discussion between the conscious parent and his child.

Balancing Time Alone

How can you be at home when you are not? This may sound like a riddle, but it isn't. When outside commitments, particularly jobs, pull parents away, a child is often left at home alone. School's out for the day, or for the summer, but you still have to be at your job during the day. Unless you invest in an afterschool program or camp, your child will probably end up at home alone at some point. At what age you should begin allowing your child to stay at home without adult supervision should be determined by local laws and regulations, your child's maturity, and your personal comfort level.

The time between the end of the school day and when parents arrive home can give a child left alone plenty of opportunities to get into trouble. It's not that this freedom is so pleasurable that the child gets into trouble. In most cases, trouble occurs because the opposite is true. This weekday freedom can be painful. It can be even more painful during long vacations.

TOO MUCH TIME ALONE?

How can freedom be painful? The answer is boredom. The problem with too much time alone is boredom—the child has more freedom than he knows how to fill. Having "nothing to do" creates a serious state of discomfort for many children. This discomfort is a kind of loneliness stemming from not being able to entertain or accompany oneself in a satisfying way. "I don't know what to do with myself!"

If you don't set some terms of safety and responsibility for keeping your child directed when you are away and he is home alone, your child will set his own terms, which may not be to your liking. "Home alone" is freedom that requires supervision.

Boredom is painful for a child because boredom feels lonely. The child is at a loss for how to connect with himself in a satisfying way. "I hate being bored!" "I hate having nothing to do!" These are true statements about true pain. It is to escape the pain of boredom that many children turn to trouble. Boredom is a staging area for trouble where children play follow-the-leader because of the impulse to find something to fill the void of emptiness they feel.

INCREASING PARENTAL PRESENCE

The danger of protracted boredom is stated strongly here to give parents warning. Don't leave your children at home alone with nothing to do. Create a supervisory parental presence for your child when you can't be there with him. After school before you get home, on the weekend, over vacation—whenever your child is left at home alone—give him some things to do that not only keep him busy but also remind him that he is still accountable to you for his behavior. Give him:

O A schedule to follow

O Activities to engage his interest

O Tasks that you approve and he enjoys

O Some household chores to accomplish

O Personal work requirements, like homework, to get done

O Specific times to communicate with you

O Specific times to expect communication from you

For safety's sake, telling the child what to do is as important as telling the child what not to do (no friends over without a parent there, or no cooking, for example). Posting the requirements, rules, and schedule for time home alone is a good idea. The poster represents the parental presence. Obviously, when your child uses this alone time well, you want to praise this show of responsibility.

The Messy Room

When your child hits early adolescence (around the ages of nine to thirteen), the freedom to keep a "messy room" often becomes an issue between parents and child. The disorderly room often feels like an affront to parents (and even more so to stepparents) who want a more orderly space in which to live. Firmly remind your youngster who pays the rent or mortgage. When she is on her own, she can keep her place however she wants.

SUPERVISING THE ENFORCEMENT OF YOUR RULES

By insisting on regular room cleanup, you let it be known that your child must live on your terms as long as she is dependent on your care. You are letting your child know that a "trashed" room causes you to feel that your home is being trashed, and you won't have that because you work to keep a home clean and in good shape. If your child knows you will continue asking for the small responsibilities such as cleaning up a messy room, she will also know that you will pursue her for big stuff such as obedience to major rules.

Now your child has a suggestion. "Just close the door and keep out and the mess won't bother you." Don't accept that offer. If you allow the child's mess to keep you and your supervision out, your child may start keeping things in the room, and conducting activities in the room, that you do not want in your home or in the child's life. At the age of awakening curiosity about the grown-up world, such freedom can be abused—as license to explore and experiment with the forbidden.

Remember that if you have a child with a high degree of ADD/ADHD characteristics, having a simplified and orderly personal space to live in can help that child gain better control over the conduct of her life, because a messy room only adds chaos to a life that is already hard to keep organized.

If your child asserts, "This is my room and you can't come in without my permission," your answer needs to be "Yes" and "No." Yes, you should knock before entering if the door is closed. Yes, you should allow the room to reflect the changing identity of your growing child (decoration within your tolerance for acceptable expression). And yes, you should value this decoration as a window into understanding your child's changing interests and identifications as she continues to grow.

This said, you also have to state conditions under which you will say no to the right of privacy. As you do with freedom for electronic communication, so do with freedom of personal space. Privacy remains a privilege, not a right. Use privacy to conceal or conduct the forbidden, and that privilege is lost because personal freedom is being abused. If your child is inexplicably changing for the worse at home and is getting into significant trouble at school or out in the world, but she refuses to discuss with you what is happening, asserting your right of "search and seizure" in her room may uncover private communications or paraphernalia that disclose what is really going on.

Resisting Schoolwork

As children enter adolescence between the ages of nine and thirteen, they start to assert more independence and test the limits of your authority. Of course, every child is a unique individual, but in the process of this change, it is very common for a child who previously was very motivated academically to slack off doing his schoolwork in favor of spending more time focusing on the social aspects of his life—connecting with friends and being popular. Energy that used to be invested in doing homework is now diverted to talking long hours on the telephone and to instant messaging or texting. In consequence, less interest in accomplishing schoolwork can lead to lower grades.

In most cases, this performance drop doesn't really mean the adolescent no longer values doing well academically; it just means he doesn't want to do the work to do well—class work, homework, reports, projects, papers, and studying for tests. So it is at this juncture that parents often find themselves confronted by a number of anti-achievement behaviors. The most common ones are:

○ Not delivering deficiency notes sent home to parents, or intercepting them in the mail

○ "Forgetting" or lying about homework assignments

○ Not turning in completed homework

○ Not finishing class work

○ Being disruptive by socially talking out and acting out in class

If you establish the idea at a younger age that homework is your child's job, just as your job is to earn money for the family, there will be less argument. Also, make yourself minimally available to help with homework. You can encourage, but not get too involved. Otherwise it becomes *your* homework, and you're busy enough already.

KNOWING WHAT NOT TO DO

All these misbehaviors are very easily remedied by parents who are willing to take a stand for the adolescent's best interests against what he wants. Two things to avoid, however, are becoming emotionally upset or resorting to rewards or punishments to encourage different choices. Although both techniques can work with a young child who wants to please and who will work for material incentives, they tend to be counterproductive with the adolescent, who often courts parental disapproval to accredit independence and may resent your efforts to control those things that he wants.

Grades are too important to get emotionally upset about. Growth is just a gathering of power; from dependence to independence, the job of parents is to help their adolescent gather that power in appropriate ways. It is not appropriate for parents to give the adolescent power to get them upset over grades, because then the academic focus is lost and the young person wins influence over parental feelings. "I can really push my parents' buttons by doing poorly in school."

Grades are too important to reward or punish. Parents often mistakenly believe that offering an adolescent some significant payoff for good grades will be seen as a reward. But by this age, the time when earning systems can work is over. In fact, most adolescents will see it as a threat that they resent. "If you say you're going to give me five dollars for an A, that just means that if I don't get an A, I don't get the five dollars."

Getting upset over grades turns a performance issue into an emotional encounter, showing the adolescent that he can control your emotions by his willingness to work or not work at school.

Likewise, taking away some resource or freedom until grades improve usually just makes the child resist more than cooperate. "I don't care what you take away, you can't make me do my work!" When parents reward or punish grades, they turn a performance issue into a power struggle with their adolescent.

The Power of Supervision

So, your thirteen-year-old is suddenly refusing to do her homework. What's a parent to do? Just stand by and watch her early adolescent fail from failing to do the work? Sometimes that's the advice middle-school teachers give to parents. "Don't be overprotective. Let your child fail and learn responsibility from the consequences." But unless the adolescent has the maturity to correct herself, buckling down to bring her grades up, she will only learn to adjust to failure, treating situations like this as okay when they are not.

After all, a report card is meant to act like a mirror, the adolescent seeing in that written evaluation an adequate reflection of her capacities. Parents saying to an unmotivated adolescent who is capable of As and Bs, "All we want you to do is pass," is tantamount to giving up on their child, withdrawing faith in her high potential, and abandoning their responsibility to influence school behavior. But if emotional upset and rewards and punishments tend to be ineffective with the early adolescent achievement drop, then what are parents to do?

The answer is supervision—pursuit and surveillance. Remember that the early adolescent, unlike the child, does not want parents showing up in her world at school. Desire for social independence means keeping parents out of her society of peers. Now the company of parents at school feels like a public embarrassment because she should be able to handle school without their interference. To which parents reply, "We have no desire to interfere at school as long as you are taking care of business. However, if you do not do schoolwork and if you are acting inappropriately in class, we will extend our supervision into your school to help you make better choices."

If deficiency notices are not delivered at home, you may want to say something like this: "Since information for us that the school entrusted to you was not delivered, we will meet with the teacher together, and you will have the opportunity to explain why the notice failed to reach us and what you are going to do differently next time so it does."

If your child has told you she had no homework when she really did, you may want to say something like this: "Since you said you had no homework, but you did, we will meet with the teacher together. At that time, you will have the opportunity to explain why you said there was no homework when there was, and what you will do differently the next time so we will be told the truth. And this weekend, before you get to do anything you want to do, you will have to complete the missed assignments, turning them in for zero credit because they are now late." And if homework still is not reliably brought home, you promise to meet your child at the end of the last class and together make the rounds of the teachers to pick up all homework.

If the adolescent does the homework but chooses not to turn it in, you may want to say something like this: "Since you can't manage to turn your work in, we will go up to school with you and walk the halls together and make the rounds of all your teachers to make sure your homework gets turned in."

Doing homework is more important than practicing a given subject. By faithfully doing their homework, children are learning to develop a work ethic—the ability to make themselves complete what they started, a discipline that will serve them well in later life.

If the adolescent is talking out or acting out disruptively in class, or not completing teacher assignments, you may want to say something like this: "Although this is not something we want to do, we are willing to take time off from work and sit together with you in class to help you behave appropriately as the teacher asks."

Usually, an early adolescent will not welcome any of these options, considering them outrageously invasive, preferring to correct self-defeating conduct instead. What you are saying in each case, however, is that as long as self-correction does not occur, you are committed to steadfast supervision because you know improved school performance will ultimately cause the adolescent to feel better about herself, as well as keep choices open in the future.

Supervision shows your child that you care enough to keep after her with pursuit and surveillance so she takes care of responsibilities that are in her best interests to accomplish. Supervision (nagging and checking) is honorable work and needs to be faithfully done.

Behavior Snapshot

Supervision is a necessary part of parenting. Trust is earned; when your child proves that he can make good choices, he gets more freedom, and when he makes bad choices, the pursuit continues.

What happens: Your middle-school child calls you at work, as agreed, when he is home from school. His call is a little later than usual on this particular day. He opens the conversation with the statement "I got most of the smoke out."

What you *want* to do: Call the fire department, leave work, and save the building and your child from a towering inferno.

What you should do: Calmly ask questions and listen to the answers. You learn that your child attempted to warm up some food in the oven and it burned, smoking up the apartment. He got busy with homework and forgot about the food. You reassure him that he did the right thing to tell you. You tell him to turn off the oven and open the windows.

Important Points to Consider

Supervision, while not always fun, is necessary as a parent. The act of supervision is made up of equal parts pursuit and surveillance. Here are some points to consider regarding supervision:

O Supervision, though sometimes annoying for both the parent and the child, actually shows that you care.

O Lack of supervision can lead to both physical and emotional harm.

O Sometimes, relentless reminding is necessary to demonstrate that a task must be completed.

O While providing choices for an activity is ideal, some tasks, such as chores and personal safety practices, are non-negotiable.

CHAPTER 12

Punishment: The Third Factor

Punishment can certainly be persuasive. Applying a negative consequence can discourage repetition of wrongdoing. "I had to work to earn the money to pay for replacing the window I broke, so I'm going to stop throwing the ball around inside the house." When practiced intentionally, it can teach valuable lessons. As effective as some punishments are, there is little benefit to physical punishment. Spanking demonstrates that when you are bigger than another person, it's okay to hit him to release your anger or to get your way. Spanking teaches that hitting is okay.

Violence Teaches Violence

"Do as I say and not as I do" simply doesn't fly with children. Physical punishment should never be used to discipline. Children should not learn that hitting is a way to solve problems. This has serious ramifications for their future relationships.

There are other kinds of nonviolent negative consequences you can enforce. The point is to encourage the child to think about why the consequence has been imposed and to consider not committing that significant misbehavior again.

There are situations where you might feel so angry or frustrated that it elicits a physical response. When emotions impact you physically, it can be tempting to respond by hitting, throwing, or lashing out. Recognizing the severity of your anger, and making the effort to control your response, sets a positive example for your child. A time out, for both parent and child, can ease tension and prevent you and your child from resorting to violence.

Good Parents Never Back Off

Constructive punishment is a discipline tactic that you should reserve for violations of significant family rules and agreements. It is designed to catch the child's attention, cause her to rethink what happened, and discourage her from committing that forbidden action again. "Because I stole some money from my mom's purse, I not only have to pay her back, but I also have to keep her purse in my room at night, count out to her how much money it contains before I go to bed, and repeat the count the next morning to make sure no money is missing before giving it back to her. And I have to do this for two weeks! She doesn't want me to forget what I did wrong. She wants me to learn to be trustworthy around her money." The purpose of punishment is to use a negative consequence to teach the child what not to do again.

Good punishment is an art. Like the example just given, it can be creative, where parents design a consequence that demonstrates exactly what they don't want to happen again, and by implication what they do. In this case, they want trustworthy behavior regarding the parents' money.

> The purpose of punishment is never to cause physical or emotional injury. The purpose is to apply a consequence that has enough symbolic value that it convinces the child not to repeat this offense again.

TESTING RULES

To some degree, the relationship between parent and child is between rule maker and rule breaker. In adolescence this can become a kind of serious game, with the teenager testing rules, getting around rules, and disobeying rules to gain more freedom while parents, in the interests of their child's safety and responsibility, monitor compliance and respond to violations that occur.

Children grow up partly within and partly outside their parents' rules. No child is 100 percent obedient or tells parents the whole truth all the time. For parents, significant compliance and adequate communication are the best compromise they are going to get.

Sometimes in ignorance, sometimes on impulse, sometimes under the influence of friends, sometimes under the influence of substances, sometimes with deliberate intent, your child will break one of your rules. Just as you reward compliance with appreciation and more freedom, you penalize serious infractions with punishment.

> Parents who regularly punish or threaten punishment to get routine consent punish too much. To be effective, punishment must be selective. The more often punishment is used, the less corrective power it has. "Big deal, you're going to ground me from watching TV again."

THE EMOTIONAL SIDE

Even when a major rule has been violated, you may be tempted not to apply punishment for a couple of reasons. First, your child will feel unhappy receiving the consequence, and you may want to avoid causing that unhappiness because you can't stand making your child "feel sad." And second, feeling unhappy about a punishment she doesn't like or doesn't agree with, the child may decide to punish you back with disapproval or anger. "I'm never going to like or talk to you again. Ever!" To avoid this punishment from your child, you may prefer to let the violation go. In the first case, you don't want to cause your child pain; in the second, you don't want to receive pain yourself. Good parents need to be clear about the difference between rules and guidelines. Always follow through if it really is a rule.

The Power of Enforcement

When the child is young and small and helpless, it is particularly hard for parents to be careful when they exercise their authority and not abuse the greater size and strength that they possess. To some degree, most parents will occasionally abuse their adult power by allowing fatigue, frustration, or impatience to result in a raised voice, threatening words, or an angry touch. How can these responses be abusive to your child? Because they can scare the child, and fear of parents violates the child's sense of safety with the people on whom he most depends for love and care.

THE PROBLEM WITH FEAR

Punishment is a strong exercise of corrective power. It demonstrates how significantly a parent can affect conditions in a child's life. The purpose of punishment is to teach a lesson, not to make a child afraid. This is why punishment must be decided rationally, not emotionally. If you choose to enforce rules by using punishment to instill fear, you may get strict obedience, but it will be at excessive cost. Your child will learn to:

O Distrust you because you are not safe.

O Keep his distance from you in order to be safe.

O Manipulate you with dishonesty in order to keep safe.

O Love you less as he comes to fear you more.

Using intimidation to influence obedience can be at the expense of closeness now and friendship later as adult children may remain distant, resenting the parent who once ruled their life by exploiting their fear.

THE PROBLEM WITH ANGER

Unless you express your anger separately from the punishment you give ("I'm going to tell you how angry I am now, and later we'll discuss the consequence for what you did"), you are likely to overreact and overpunish. Allowing emotion to do your thinking for you, you will declare a punishment that is either too extreme or unenforceable, having to later retract or modify it, which shows that you didn't really mean what you said in the first place: "You're grounded for the next year!"

Being angry is perfectly normal. If you (or your child) didn't get angry from time to time, that could indicate a serious problem. When acknowledged, accepted, and managed, anger can be a powerful motivator. When it's uncontrolled and used to punish, it can be a divider. In the moment, anger over what is "wrong" can obscure appreciation of all that is "right." For young children, parental anger is threatening for this reason. Because an angry parent seems not to be a loving parent, it takes some learning for the child to understand that such anger is only a passing interruption, and that parental love is here to stay.

WHAT ANGER TEACHES CHILDREN

To be punished by an angry parent causes the child to associate his parent's anger with being treated in a powerfully aversive way. "Stop playing and go sit in the corner!" yells the parent, furious after tripping over a toy that shouldn't have been left at the bottom of the stairs. "And don't you dare get up until I tell you!" When punishment is linked with anger, fear of the parent's anger can be what the child learns.

Particularly with children under six, you must remember how much physically larger and more powerful you are than they, and how important being safely attached to you is for their emotional security. Larger size amplifies the power of parental anger.

Very young children can be frightened by parental anger or their own: Where did loving feelings go and will they return? It takes repeated safe experiences to trust that anger does not destroy love; it only temporarily interrupts the flow of loving feelings. This is why anger over a disciplinary violation needs to be expressed safely by talking it out and not acting it out. Far better for parents to explain anger by verbally describing their feelings in response to what occurred than by acting those angry feelings out in criticism, threats, yelling, or temper.

> Punishment and anger don't always get along. Punishment is a time for due deliberation to select an appropriate consequence that will deter some wrongdoing from happening again. Waiting to find out what the consequence will be is part of the punishment.

When it comes to managing anger at your child for misbehavior, keep your hands to yourself.

○ Never lay angry hands on your child to get his attention.

○ Never use angry hands to "shake some sense" into your child or to express your frustration.

○ Never use angry hands to threaten physical harm.

For the parent of an adolescent, anger can sometimes be sticky. After unsuccessfully trying to settle a disagreement with an obstinate teenager, anger can stick around because the angry parent is holding on to it, refusing to let go. "Even though it's over, every time I think about the argument with my son, I still feel angry! He just wouldn't see things my way! And he wouldn't let me have the last word!"

ARE YOU AN ANGER-PRONE PARENT?

Anger is functional. It is a healthy response to perceived violations of your well-being. It empowers you to make an expressive, corrective, or protective response. "When you use sarcastic name-calling to put me down, I feel hurt and angry. As your parent, I don't do that with you, and I don't want you doing it with me."

But what if you or your family feels that you are angry too much of the time? You may be anger prone if you have one or more of the following characteristics.

○ The more controlling you are, the angrier you will get when you do not get your way right away. A child's delay will be treated as an act of defiance.

○ The more judgmental you are, the angrier you will get at those who do "wrong" in your eyes, or who refuse to accept that you are "right." A child's disagreement will be treated as an act of disrespect.

○ The more sensitive to hurt you are, the angrier you will get at unintended offenses from others. A child's forgetfulness will be treated as a personal affront.

Anger-prone parents tend to train a child to become anger-prone like themselves, or to become someone who grows up frightened of anger, avoiding or placating other people's anger to his personal cost.

If you hold on to anger too long, it will turn into resentment, doing you much more harm than it does the child at whom you're still angry. Anger can be toxic to the holder.

If you are prone to one or more of these characteristics, either at home or behind the wheel of a car with a child as passenger, work on changing them. You can change them with practice. Tell yourself, "I don't have to take offense at what I don't like if I don't want to." Discipline is most effective when it is free from anger.

The Limits of Punishment

Punishment should be used only to enforce major rule violations, not to correct continuing irritations (such as not picking up clothes, leaving the refrigerator door open, playing music too loud) or minor infractions (such not doing chores, continuing to talk on the phone after hours, not doing homework). These more minor instances of misbehavior should not be dealt with by punishment since they are guidance and supervisory issues. Lying, sneaking out, hitting another person, stealing, driving under the influence of substances, skipping school—these are the kinds of choices that constitute major violations that may require punishment as a corrective.

DEFEATING THE PURPOSE

Although not a part of instruction, as a correction, punishment is still meant to reform misbehavior. It should not be used to inflict physical or emotional injury. Parents who use sarcasm to embarrass, who use humiliation to shame, who use criticism to devalue, who use temper to intimidate, who use suffering to arouse guilt, or who use anger to inflict bodily harm are not only destructive but they are self-defeating as well. For punishment to be corrective, it needs to be rationally thought out, not emotionally driven.

Parents are most at risk of losing control of themselves when they feel they are powerless to affect their child. In reality, no parent is 100 percent without influence, because no child is 100 percent uncooperative. Parents always have some platform of positive influence to build on because the child is always doing some things they want and is not always doing some things they don't want.

When it comes to punishment, knowing what not to do is as important as knowing what you should do. Don't punish to get back at your child, to get even with your child, to make your child feel bad, to show your child who's boss, to relieve your frustration, or to satisfy your anger.

PHYSICAL PUNISHMENT

Although many parents would deny it, physical punishment is given more often for the parent's sake (to relieve frustration or take out anger) than it is given for the child's sake (to discourage repetition of misbehavior). In general, physical punishment such as poking, pinching, squeezing, spanking, swatting, popping, slapping, and belting proves only four things to the child: "You are bigger. You are stronger. You are entitled to be violent. And when I'm a grown-up, I will be entitled to act the same way."

The means (the physical hurt), not the end (learning not to repeat the offense), becomes the major message. "All I learned is that because he is bigger and stronger, my dad can slap me around!"

Add up all the arguments for spanking, and together they do not outweigh this one objection against it. Spanking teaches the child that hitting is okay if you are bigger and stronger and cannot get what you want any other way. Spanking teaches hitting.

External and Natural Consequences

Because your child spends time outside the family system, there are external rules that he must follow as well. There are social laws and school regulations, for example, and when they are violated, official authorities may apply punitive consequences such as arresting a teenager for public misbehavior or requiring a child to serve detention for skipping school.

There are also natural consequences that arise when a child's choice leads to an unintended outcome that punishes the original decision that was made. A thoughtless or careless decision can lead to a punitive outcome. Thus, a wallet carelessly left out in the locker room at school is missing after athletic practice. The adolescent has been taught a lesson on taking care of personal belongings.

As a general rule, don't double-punish misbehavior when your child has already suffered external consequences enforced by other authorities or has experienced adverse natural consequences. Instead, sympathetically help your child learn from what occurred.

Of course, there are exceptions to the general rule of not double punishing when external or natural negative consequences have already occurred. For example, if your adolescent gets charged with a DWI (driving while intoxicated), you certainly want him to experience whatever legal, educational, and community service consequences apply. In addition, however, you may also want to take away or restrict driving privileges until your child can demonstrate that he can be more responsible about using the car. In this case, the external consequence is not punishment enough.

At home, there are three kinds of punishment parents can use that have different kinds of corrective power: isolation, deprivation, and reparation.

Isolation As Punishment

Isolation is temporary exclusion. The most common form of isolation is taking a time-out. The purpose of isolation is not to ostracize or reject the child. It simply separates the child from a problem situation and begins a process to help the child commit to correcting misbehavior so she can behave acceptably in the family once again. A time-out is often helpful for children of all ages, and for adults as well.

> Children learn from experience only when they accept the consequences of their decisions. They won't learn from consequences as long as they deny responsibility for personal choice or parents deal with those consequences for them.

EFFECTIVE TIME-OUTS

After getting the child out of the problem situation, a time-out should last only however long as is needed for the child to be willing to calm down, think out, and then talk out what happened and what she will do differently from now on. So, after your daughter has grabbed the remote control from her younger brother (whose turn it was to select a TV program) and hit him when he objected, you give her a time-out to think about what she did. She violated the family rules against taking and hitting. When she feels she has calmed down, has thought about the incident enough, and feels ready, the girl lets the parent know she is ready for discussion. This means she feels ready and willing to talk about what happened, why it happened, and what she's going to do differently the next time so this misbehavior doesn't happen again.

Fully discussing what happened helps to further develop talking-out skills, which may then be used to work out solutions in the future instead of just acting out objections. Of course, once the time-out sequence has been completed, you should make sure a positive focus on the child and your relationship has been restored.

KEEPING EMOTIONS UNDER CONTROL

Time-outs also serve another purpose. When you or your child, or both of you, are getting too emotionally intense about an issue in a disagreement, declare a mutual time-out to cool both of you down. The purpose of this time-out is to reduce emotional arousal, restore perspective, and then reopen the discussion, both of you now prepared to "start over" in a more reasonable manner. During this cooling-off period, you have each had a chance to think up some new ways of approaching the issue at difference between you.

Deprivation As Punishment

Deprivation is passive punishment. Deprivation is a strategy for taking away a usual access or social freedom the child values as a consequence of his having done a major wrong. Access usually has to do with the privilege of using such things as the computer, the telephone, the TV, or the car. Freedom has to do with the permission to socialize on normal terms with friends or engage in normal outside activities.

The timing of taking either privilege or permission away is important. In some cases, long periods of deprivation can lessen their hold on a child. For this reason, deprivation time should be considered carefully. Taking away the privilege of watching a favorite TV program for twelve weeks could end up with a child losing interest and finding a new pastime. Taking away something that a child feels he cannot live without, like Internet access, can often be very effective, even if it's for a short period of time. Never use deprivation to take away any outside activity that serves as a pillar of the child's self-esteem, such as church youth group activities or sports.

Sometimes when a parent feels overwhelmed, she will strip the child of everything he values doing to show how serious (or angry) she is. Extreme deprivation is a big mistake. Now the child has nothing left to lose, so there is no reason to stop the behavior (unless he's been clearly told how to earn the items back).

GROUNDING IN

Deprivation of freedom, or "grounding," is usually used with adolescents who are at the age of growing up when social freedom matters most of all. Grounding can include prohibition against going out with friends, against having friends over, against talking on the phone, against computer messaging with friends, or against engaging in normal social or recreational activities. Long-term grounding tends to be counterproductive because you turn punishment into a prison sentence, your home into a prison, your child into a prisoner, and yourself into a prison guard as grounded as the prisoner you keep. Over a sustained time, you will both learn only to resent each other.

Long-term grounding in also can have a social cost you do not want your child to pay. If you take your child out of social action in his peer group long enough, the child will lose standing in that social order. On returning, he must struggle to reclaim a place that may have been taken by someone else, and now your child will be more subject to peer pressure than was the case before.

GROUNDING OUT

In extreme cases, there is another kind of grounding, different from "grounding in." Suppose your late adolescent refuses to stay grounded in the house for violating curfew and decides he can leave home anytime he likes and stay gone as long as he wants. At this time, you may elect to use "grounding out."

You say something like this to your unruly teenager: "You need to know that we are operating a home, not a prison. As you have made perfectly clear, you can leave whenever you choose and stay out as late as you like. We can't stop you. However, although leaving is up to you, permission to return is up to us. When you want to return, you can call us. From the time of that phone call, you must stay away from home twelve hours for the first curfew infraction, twenty-four hours for the next curfew infraction, and so on. During that time you will have to make your own living arrangements, and you cannot come by and pick up clothes or any other belongings. At the end of this grounding out, we will meet you at an outside location at a time of our convenience to discuss the rules you must be willing to live by if you want to return to live at home."

This is an extreme measure and should be considered carefully. As you can imagine, "grounding out" does not promote the development of close relationships; however, for some late adolescents and for those working their way through trial independence, this is an option to consider.

Reparation As Punishment

Reparation is active punishment. "Because you did something you weren't supposed to do, you will have to work off the infraction before you get to do anything else you want to do." There are a number of advantages to using reparation as a punishment.

- O The child has to actively do something to work off the infraction.

- O While working off the infraction, the child has time to think about the violation that led to this consequence.

- O When the infraction is worked off, the child goes forward with a clean record, confident that the particular infraction has been paid for and will not be brought up by parents against her again.

Sometimes parents will keep a list of usual household jobs (not regular chores) that need to be done posted on the refrigerator that can be referred to when they need to apply a punishment. "You need to get this job done to our satisfaction before you are allowed to pursue anything else you want to do that requires our assistance, support, or permission." Reparation can be creative in terms of the punishment fitting the crime. Imagine that you live in an urban area, and you learn that your teenager was involved in tagging the side of the building owned by a local laundromat. You take your teenager to speak with the owner and work out an arrangement for the wall to be repainted by your teenager.

The Negative Attention Trap

It's not just that positive parental attention has more power to shape positive behavior in a child than negative parental attention does, but excessive negative attention can help make some misbehavior immeasurably worse.

MISBEHAVING FOR ATTENTION

Consider the following situation. Despite his father's nightly warnings about not spilling at supper, the child manages to spill something at least once a week, causing the father to regularly lose his temper in response. "What's the matter with you? What do I have to do to get you to watch what you're doing?"

Then, after the child has been sent from the table, the father wonders, "Why does he keep spilling when he knows how upset I get?" Of course, the father's answer is in his question. That's why the child spills: to get a lot of negative attention from his father.

Why would a child want negative attention?

O Negative attention feels better than no attention.

O By his reacting so predictably when the child spills, the child gains apparent control over his father's behavior.

O There is a sense of power in being stubbornly uncorrectable.

CHANGING NEGATIVE FOCUS INTO POSITIVE FOCUS

Actually, if the father had kept a clearer focus, he could have discovered the motivation behind his child's behavior. The key to his understanding is that, in anger, he believed the boy spilled "every night," but on emotionally sober reflection, he realized that some nights, like last night, he doesn't spill. Why not? What contact did he and the boy have before supper? For whatever reason, last night he had the energy to play a game before they sat down to eat. Maybe, because he was given positive attention to begin with, the child didn't need to provoke bad attention in the end.

Critical parents, who find it easier to get angry than to give approval, are easily caught in negative attention traps.

Although the child is used to getting angry attention from his dad, the boy will quickly prefer getting loving attention from him instead. When it comes to parental attention, negative may feel better than no attention, but positive feels better than negative.

Behavior Snapshot

Punishment is necessary when major rules are broken. Though enforcing punishment is rarely pleasant, punishment can be a valuable teaching tool for your child.

What happens: At a family holiday dinner your teenager persists in texting during the meal, when you specifically asked her not to do that in the presence of relatives and other guests.

What you *want* to do: Scream at her for the apparent defiance of your request.

What you should do: Without saying a word, quietly take the phone from her hand, leave the room, and place the phone somewhere for safekeeping until the meal is finished.

Important Points to Consider

When given appropriately, punishment can be a powerful motivator for change. Here are some important points to consider about punishment:

O Appropriate punishment can take three forms: isolation, deprivation, and reparation.

O Punishments that result from feelings of anger are rarely effective.

O Negative attention-seeking is often the result of an underlying need for attention.

 **CHAPTER 13**

Exchange Points: The Fourth Factor

Of the four basic discipline techniques, using exchange points has the most training value. Its immediate benefit to the child is teaching that there is a connection between getting what she wants and giving her parents what they want. Furthermore, it helps the child understand how to conduct healthy relationships in the future. Children depend on a parent for a great deal of support that they take for granted. They believe that providing resources, permission, help, and a variety of services is what a parent is "supposed" to do.

Good Parents Get As Well As Give

For parents, the idea of "all give and no get" can feel tiresome at best and exploitative at worst. With this tendency in mind, children may become used to a one-way relationship where they do most of the getting and the parent does most of the giving. As far as children are concerned, that's fine.

So when children make a request or expect to be provided some service, the parent makes sure that an exchange takes place. "I am certainly willing to drive you over to your friend's home, but before we go, I want ten minutes of your help folding the laundry." This is an exchange point: When you do something for your child and your child does something for you in return. It tells the child now and teaches her for later that giving in relationships goes two ways, not just one.

When parents use an exchange point to withhold what the child wants until they get what they want, they are not being punitive, because they aren't being negative or threatening to take anything away. Using exchange points is positive: "I will be glad to do what you want after you have done something for me."

Your child may protest, "I promise I'll bring in the trash like you asked when we get back. Can't we go now?" No. Unless the child has proven extremely faithful about keeping agreements, you may want to treat promises as false currency. It is performance that counts. "First the trash; then the ride."

Anytime your child asks or expects something of you, there is a potential for an exchange point. Ask yourself, "Was there something I requested from my child that has not yet been given?" If so, don't give until you get. "I'm glad you're here on time for supper, but before you sit down to eat please pick up your backpack from the hall and put it in your room like I asked."

Without some give-and-take by both parties, an unhappy disparity can grow within a caring relationship. When one party does most of the giving while the other party does most of the taking, the giver is likely to start building resentment toward the taker.

Consider chores, those regular household tasks that your adolescent regularly puts off as long as possible. You've tried guidance, explaining why you need chores done in a timely way, and words have proven ineffective. You've tried supervision and pursuit to get chores done, and that has proved exhausting. You don't believe delaying chores is a major rule violation, so you are not going to waste the big gun of punishment on a small but persistent aggravation.

Instead, you just wait until the next exchange point. Because of all the ways your teenager is dependent on you, it will come around soon enough. And when it does, you let your child know how happy you will be to do what is wanted, but not until the chore you wanted done has been accomplished first. Good parents get as well as give.

The Power of Mutuality

Beyond getting what you want at the moment, using exchange points teaches your child to practice mutuality in the relationships that matter to him. Mutuality involves making three basic exchanges.

O **Reciprocity:** This means that each party contributes to the other's well-being. So your child has been trained not only to receive help from you, but to give help to you as well.

O **Compromise:** Both parties must be willing to sacrifice some self-interest for each other and for the greater good of their relationship. Your child has been trained to cooperate by giving up some wants to get along with you, just like you do with your child.

O **Consideration:** Both parties must make an effort to be respectful of each other's sensitivities. So your child has been trained to not knowingly go after your emotional sore points, those issues about which you are easily hurt, just as you avoid sore points with your child.

With this training in mutuality in place, your child is not only appreciated at home, but is also usually well received out in the world, where his interpersonal skills will help him create and sustain two-way relationships with other people.

SOMEONE YOU CAN ENJOY LIVING WITH

Children who have practiced and acquired the three exchanges of mutuality are generally nice for parents to live with, and nice for others to interact with out in the world. But what about children who have not been trained this way? What about those children who have been trained to believe in one-way relationships? What about children who have been trained by insecure, compliant, indulgent, or neglectful parenting to believe that all the benefits in a relationship should go their way? What about children who have modeled themselves after a parent who mostly gets and takes at home, but rarely gives? In those cases, you get a child who is no pleasure for parents to live with.

> One goal for parents is to raise a nice child—one who, for the most part, they enjoy being around because she has been trained by their discipline to live in a two-way relationship with them.

One of the risks of adolescence, when children typically become extremely preoccupied with their own needs and become more intent on satisfying personal wants, is that parents may allow training in mutuality to lapse. When they do, they get a teenager committed to one-way behavior: "My needs come first," "Things should be done my way," and "My feelings matter more than anyone else's." Unless you want to live with a teenager who believes these statements and acts on these beliefs, you had better insist that the three exchanges of mutuality be met all the way through the teenage years.

Predictable Behaviors in Parents

Sometimes you may become stuck in a negative exchange with your child. There's giving and getting, all right, but you're not happy with the exchange. Lately, whenever you refuse to let your teenager do what he wants, he gets angry, gets in your face, raises his voice, and loudly demands that you change your mind. The question is, why does he act this way? The answer may be the same as the answer to this question: "What does he predict you will do in response?"

If you want to change this exchange, you may choose to react in a different way than he expects. To do this, first identify what your specific behaviors are when you react to his aggressive challenge to your refusal of his request. Suppose, on reflection, you can name three: you stop talking, you feel your facial expression become tense with fright, and you back away. Maybe you even back off your decision. These behaviors are part of what he predicts will happen—he knows that by getting in your face he can intimidate you. He is getting the response he wants in this exchange.

Now you decide to change your reaction. The next time you refuse a request and he gets in your face angrily and loudly, you choose to act very differently. You smile, you put your hands on his shoulders, you pull him toward you, you kiss him on the cheek, and you start telling him how much you love him when he acts this way. Instead of showing him intimidation, you are giving him affection. And you let your decision stand.

Wow! This is not the response he was predicting or working for. If this is how you're going to act when he gets in your face, maybe he won't get in your face again, because this is not the response he wanted.

Taking Back the Initiative

Sometimes the exchange between parent and child becomes one-sided in terms of who initiates most interactions in the relationship. For example, parents describe the relationship with their prickly adolescent like this: "We're always waiting to see what she's going to do next. When she comes home from school, is she going to act pleasant or unpleasant, be in a good mood or bad mood, like us or criticize us, do what we ask or refuse? We get so nervous around her, not knowing what to expect. We're the parents, but she's really in charge."

Mutuality means that both you and your child share the responsibility (and the rewards) of taking initiative in the relationship.

The parents are correct. Their daughter has begun to control the initiative in their exchange. They allow her actions to keep them constantly on the reactive. Essentially, she dictates the agenda and focus in the relationship. The question these parents continually ask themselves is "What does she want from us now?" The question they need to start asking themselves is "What do we want from her now?"

When this kind of imbalance in the exchange with their child takes place, parents can take back the initiative by claiming a more active role in the relationship, making more requests of their own, putting the teenager more on the reactive. As soon as your daughter storms in the door from school, instead of waiting to see what she's going to do, greet her with several pieces of family business you need from her. Your actions immediately put her on the reactive for a change.

After arguing (which you most likely predicted), she flees to her bedroom in protest, but there is no getting away. For the next week, whenever you see her, give her something you want her to do, give her feedback on something, or ask her questions about her life. Now more balance in initiative has been re-established.

Being Part of the Family

A family is a system of interpersonal relationships in which the welfare of the whole depends on contributions by its members. If no one contributed, the family would cease to function, each member simply going his or her own way. Although parents are the major contributors, children must be taught to make significant contributions as well.

Household membership requirements such as daily cooperation, chores, and helping out teach the child that to get benefits from parents there is a simple rule: no investment, no return.

If mutuality functions well in your family system, then everyone understands that relationships are supposed to work two ways and not just one. If exchanges ("I do for you; you do for me") are taken for granted as a natural part of family life, then your child is more likely to accept the principle that to get, he has to give. The lesson of mutuality you want to teach your child is that it takes a personal investment to get something from his parents (except, of course, your love and acceptance).

Parents who demand no household membership requirements only increase a child's belief that relationships are supposed to be one-way. Then they get angry with the "selfish" or "inconsiderate" or "unhelpful" child, but that anger is misplaced. They are better off getting angry with themselves for not training their child to be a stakeholder in the family system by becoming a contributing member. Ultimately, it is the child who suffers, because noncontributing children will become noncontributing adults, who often have difficulty sustaining healthy relationships.

FAMILY RITUALS

One way to develop a sense of cohesiveness within your family is to create traditions. Some families like to always attend a movie the afternoon of Thanksgiving Day. Others always have a barbecue on Labor Day. Some families have a routine of always quietly reading for a while in the evening after dinner. Part of the fun of forming a family is learning about the traditions of your partner and distilling a new set of rituals that is enjoyable for everybody. Then in future generations, your son or daughter will say, "In my family, this is how we always did it!"

Behavior Snapshot

Exchange points are a building block in the strong relationship you want to have with your child. Here is an example of using exchange points:

What happens: Your middle-school-aged daughter wants to ask a friend over during the evening on short notice. This will require some minor adjustments on your part, mainly planning for dinner and snacks later in the evening.

What you *want* to do: Say no. You're tired and would like to just relax among your family members.

What you should do: Ask your daughter to help you trim up the shrubbery around the house and carry the trimmings to the dumpster. Then she can have company.

Important Points to Consider

Recognizing that each of us, as unique individuals, has needs is part of the conscious parenting philosophy. These needs can be utilized to build cohesive family structure by using exchange points.

- O Exchange points require your child to give you something in order to get something that he wants.

- O Creating exchange points enhances the harmony within a household and prepares your child to function in the outside world.

- O Exchange points become negative when a child begins to predict negative response and display behavior that aims to achieve the desired negativity.

- O Encouraging mutuality increases the bond between family members.

 **CHAPTER 14**

Discipline Changes with Age

As your child grows older, your approaches to discipline must change in response. As your child grows up, he will develop a greater capacity for language, for understanding, for judgment, for responsibility, for spending more time away from home, and for getting into normal trouble. Just as different discipline techniques work better with different personalities, some techniques will work best with different ages.

Early Childhood (Up to Age Three)

At the outset of childhood, a child needs to feel securely attached to you, safely trusting in your love. He must be shown how to behave, because he hasn't mastered the language skills needed to learn through verbal explanation. Fortunately, it is easy to show a very young child how to behave, because he naturally imitates parental actions.

GIVING INSTRUCTION

You instruct your child how to behave through examples. Through your endlessly repetitive modeling, playing, and gaming, your child gradually acquires early disciplinary skills and understanding, such as how to clean up and how to eat. Your child wants to learn to act like you.

Patience and positive attention are the order of the day. Rewarding desirable behaviors with expressions of pleasure and praise encourages the child to repeat those behaviors, because pleasing parents is what children at this age most want to do. Thus, rewarding a desired behavior such as toilet training when it happens works far better than trying to force that behavior on a child with insistence, frustration, anger, or expressions of displeasure when it is not done. "I'm going to make him sit there until he does it!"

No single discipline technique works all the time for every parent with every child in every situation. Parents need many approaches to discipline from which to choose and must keep choosing until they find one that is effective for that particular child at that particular time.

Children are not one-trial learners. Maintaining a sense of play and having patience with practice is necessary for instruction to succeed. Reward both effort and success with positive attention. The formula for disciplinary teaching at this age is:

Play + Patience + Practice + Positive Attention = Productive Instruction

GIVING CORRECTION

Because parental displeasure, particularly anger, can be so frightening at this early age, parents need to rely as much as possible on instruction to instill discipline, turning to correction as a last resort. If, however, redirecting and re-educating is not working with your child's throwing objects or hitting, you can gently but firmly correct with a headshake "No."

BITING AND HITTING

Adults are understandably disturbed when their child bites or hits other children. This sort of primitive action arouses primitive feelings in the parents and other adults in the vicinity. What should you do? Make it evident to your child that biting and hitting are not okay. Physically remove him from the environment and restrain him from further misbehavior. This is not the time to lecture, but a simple statement such as "We are never allowed to bite or hit other people" is enough. Don't give undue attention to the offender, as it may turn into a situation where the child starts to thrive on negative reinforcement. Do what you can to restructure the environment so there is less opportunity for the mishap.

Late Childhood (Ages Four to Eight)

Once your child has acquired the power to understand speech and to speak, you can provide an enormous amount of instructional discipline through verbal description and explanation. There are all kinds of how-to skills to master that teach a host of responsible behaviors—dressing, basic hygiene, memorizing home address and phone number, doing household chores, following directions.

During this time, you begin modeling two important foundations for later discipline—cooperation and responsibility. You provide the building blocks of cooperation by training the child in listening and attending, giving to get, keeping agreements, and being of service to the family. You teach the basis of responsibility by helping your child learn the relationship between choice and consequence, connecting a decision she makes with the outcome that follows. For example, when she makes choices that you approve of, she gets a positive response from you. Likewise, if she makes a choice you do not approve of, she learns that she will receive a correction from you. "You can influence my reactions with your actions," is the lesson you now start to teach.

A time-out can be a useful intervention. It removes the errant child from the problem situation and gives her time to think about her choice, process her emotions, and consider the resulting consequence. Time-outs are also great for adults.

At this age, earning and counting systems can be powerful disciplinary tools. Earning systems give the child a way to earn specific rewards based on specific positive accomplishments. "Since you did all your chores on time this week, you have earned taking a friend out to eat this weekend." Counting systems put the child on notice with a warning that if her unwanted behavior continues for the full count of three, for example, then she will suffer a specific unwelcome consequence.

Transition Into Adolescence (Ages Nine to Ten)

Around age nine, your child starts to enter adolescence, when he'll want more personal and social freedom. You must specify under what conditions you will be willing to risk giving more independence than you currently allow. You do this by creating a freedom contract, which spells out the terms your child must meet before you'll consider granting more freedoms.

The freedom contract is explained more thoroughly in Chapter 15. In short, there are six conditions to the freedom contract, all of which must be currently satisfied before more freedom is considered.

O **Believability:** Your adolescent is giving you adequate and accurate information about what is going on in his life.

- **Predictability:** Your adolescent is keeping all agreements, promises, and commitments with you.

- **Responsibility:** Your adolescent is taking good care of business at home, at school, and out in the world.

- **Mutuality:** Your adolescent is living on two-way terms with you, doing services for you just as you do services for him.

- **Availability:** Your adolescent is willing to openly discuss any parental concerns you have at any time.

- **Civility:** Your adolescent communicates with you on respectful terms, even when you disagree.

Early and Midadolescence (Ages Nine to Fifteen)

For most parents, more frequent and more serious discipline problems begin during these first two stages of adolescence. For example, your daughter may start "forgetting" unwanted obligations, become more argumentative, test limits and rules, ignore schoolwork, delay compliance with chores, experiment with the forbidden, sneak out after hours, and lie. In response, accept that these behaviors are a natural byproduct of her intense feelings, and utilize a variety of disciplinary responses to encourage positive behavior.

When you give instructional discipline, keep it specific by focusing on the behaviors you want or do not want to have happen. When you give corrective discipline, keep it nonevaluative: "I disagree with the choice you have made, here is why, and this is what will happen as a consequence."

There are four common strategies that can influence the kind of behavior you would like to see. First, use guidance as a persuasive technique. Through giving continual feedback to your adolescent about what is working well and not so well in her life, you provide a constant, caring reference for constructive conduct. If she misbehaves significantly, she should know that, regardless of what other consequences she suffers, she will always be accepted, but that additional responses may be warranted on your part. Your continual feedback operates as a compass to guide responsible decision-making.

Second, close supervision is effective discipline. Through pursuit, you will make sure that your adolescent is taking care of her responsibilities at home and at school.

Third, provide structure by setting rules—but only ones that you care enough about to back up with punishment if they're violated. Punishment is not for undone chores or homework. Those are supervisory matters. Punishment is for major rule violations. Punishments are meant to capture the teenager's attention, causing her to think about the violation and the root cause, and discourage her from repeating it again. Having to do something to work off the infraction (reparation) tends to be a more powerful corrective than simply losing a privilege or freedom (deprivation).

Lastly, use exchange points to acknowledge the teenager's dependence on parents for a host of resources, permissions, and services. The parent is basically saying "I am happy to do for you what you want, but before I do, I want you to do something for me."

These four disciplinary interventions provide larger social lessons. Throughout adult life there will be authorities telling the child what to do and what not to do, keeping after her to see that these demands are met, expecting cooperative contributions from her, and punishing infractions if social rules are violated. Family experience approximates for your child what it will be like living in the larger social system.

Late Adolescence (Ages Fifteen to Eighteen)

When the time for leaving home and living "on one's own" approaches, usually coinciding with graduation from high school, your teenager needs to be adequately equipped for managing more social freedom and responsibility than he has ever known before. The goal for parents during the late adolescent years is to prepare their teenager for this challenging transition by dedicating much of their instructional discipline during high school to imparting all the knowledge and skills he will need to successfully step off into independence, making this next step as easy as possible.

Use the late adolescent years to help your teenager acquire the varied responsibilities that support self-sufficiency. You have a lot of disciplinary work to do, and you can do it in three ways. Begin by considering what responsibilities your teenager will need to master to function more independently in the world after leaving your care. Thus, when your teenager enters late adolescence, at about the age of fifteen, ask yourself a question: "What exit responsibilities need to be in place when our teenager leaves home to successfully master more independence?" Then you list all the essential knowledge and skills you can think of that support independence.

For starters, there is hunting and interviewing for employment, creating and living on a budget, basic car maintenance, filling out an income tax form, using public transportation to get around town, and managing a debit or checking account. Having made your list, decide at what point, and through what means, during the late adolescent passage you are going to teach these skills.

Next, ask yourself another question: "What services and resources do we provide for our teenager that he can learn to provide for himself?" Explaining to your teenager what you are going to do and why, one by one you begin to transfer these responsibilities to your child, giving instruction as needed. In this fashion, your teenager now undertakes responsibilities for shopping, doing personal laundry, making personal medical and dental appointments, earning money, and paying for other personal expenses, for example.

By the end of high school, you want your teenager to be able to say "I am willing and able to take care of most of my own needs."

Finally, you focus on your teenager's final years at home to approximate the full social freedom he is soon to have after leaving home. Turn over all responsibility for schoolwork, for managing any earned and allowance money, and for nightly curfew, for example. You do this because you want to see, while your teenager is still living with you, how he manages the degree of freedom of self-determination soon to be available. If your teenager can't handle all parts of it, you want to be there to help him accept responsibility for how ill-advised choice leads to unhappy consequence.

Trial Independence (Ages Eighteen to Twenty-Three)

Living away from home and out in the world for the first time, with a host of grown-up responsibilities and commitments that must be met, the final stage of adolescence is the most challenging of all. Most young people do not find their independent footing right away. They break commitments, they struggle with responsibilities, they lack direction, and they usually make some choices that get them into trouble.

Now your disciplinary help is needed more than ever, but it needs to be only instructional, not correctional. Your daughter is too old to accept or benefit from your punishment, but is not too old to profit from what you have to teach. This openness to your instruction, however, depends on your altering your traditional role as managing parent. You have to give up that role for another: mentoring parent.

As a mentor, you are no longer in the business of trying to encourage your child to adhere to the rules of your individual household. You are not even in the business of telling her how to behave. Instead, you are someone to whom your young person, after choosing her way into trouble, can come for advice about ways to choose her way out. You are now safe to come to because you do not express disappointment, worry, criticism, anger, or despair. You are a source of ideas, of wisdom from life experience. And you are a source of empathetic and encouraging support, expressing complete confidence that your daughter has what it takes to cope with the unfortunate situation a poor choice has created, to find a way to responsibly resolve the situation, and to learn from mistakes. Mentoring is your disciplinary role during the final period of your child's growing up.

Once a Parent, Always a Parent

Even when your child is all grown up, you retain a position of influence in the young adult's life—not as corrector or instructor, but as a mentor. You continue to serve as a model for how to cope with the challenges of life. Most importantly, throughout their adult lives, be an appreciative audience, understanding support, and cheering section for all your grown children as they journey through their own challenges in life. Remember: what they wanted from you when very young, they continue to want from you when they grow older, too—affirming, attentive, approving responses to some very basic human needs.

Behavior Snapshot

How you discipline your child will change as he grows. It is through a gradual process of letting go that you will ensure that your child will be able to handle life on his own.

What happens: Your teenage son wants to spend the Christmas holiday with a friend and his family who are planning a ski vacation out of town.

What you *want* to do: Implore him to spend time with his own family as the day is coming all too soon when he will be "out of the nest." You are heartbroken that he would want to desert you during such an important time of year.

What you should do: Realize, factually, that your son is evolving into a separate person with his own social life. Recognize that this invitation is a good example that you have succeeded in raising an independent person who can make it on his own. Say that you will miss him but you want him to have a good time. Make your own plans without him, and don't call him during his time away.

Important Points to Consider

Discipline must evolve in order to meet the needs of your child and your family. Consider the following:

O The training needed by a four-year-old is not the same as the training required by a fourteen-year-old.

O Growth naturally comes with additional freedoms. By allowing your child to make choices, she will learn the benefits of positive (and negative) behaviors.

O By the time your child reaches late adolescence, your relationship should shift away from the supervisory as you take on a more consultative role.

 **CHAPTER 15**

Disciplining the Teenager

Adolescence is that ten- to twelve-year growth period that begins when your child separates from childhood around age nine to thirteen and finally graduates into early adulthood in her early to mid-twenties. It is a long process of transformation that turns a dependent child into an independent young adult. Adolescence is not a punishable offense. It is a process of growth. Therefore, do not punish teenagers for the process, but do hold them accountable for how they manage it.

Parenting the Teenager

As your child progresses through the stages of adolescence, your job as a parent is to create enough structure and guidance to help provide a safe and healthy passage through a complicated and risky period of growth. No matter how hard your daughter's childhood may have been for you, the hardest part of growing up—adolescence—comes last. Although you may spend less time with your teenage daughter than you did when she was younger, you spend much more time thinking about your child as she begins to venture out into the larger, and more dangerous, world outside of family.

Although it can be confusing to both child and parents, adolescence is an orderly process. Certain changes, tensions, conflicts, and problems tend to unfold in a predictable fashion. For example, a more negative attitude and more limit-testing come early in adolescence, followed by intense preoccupation with self and urgency for freedom by midadolescence. The desire to act like a grown-up and the anxiety of true independence are typical of late adolescence. The last phase of adolescence—trial independence—tends to be plagued by a sense of relative incompetence and a lack of direction.

As a parent you will likely become more and more disenchanted with the abrasive teenager, as your teenager will be with you. This is as it should be—conflict over freedom wears down the dependence between you until by the end of adolescence you are each willing to let the other go.

This is not to say that you are destined to experience agony when your child enters adolescence. About one-third of children seem to go through adolescence without a ripple, smoothly navigating the separation from childhood, the experimentation with becoming different, and the departure into independence all within the tolerance limits of their parents. How your child deals with the experience of adolescence will be unique to her.

The Problem of Hurry-Up Growth

As you know, some adolescents physically mature more swiftly than others do. Puberty comes early and growth changes unfold fast. Suddenly, children look several years older than other kids their age. The thirteen-year-old boy looks like a young man, or the thirteen-year-old girl looks like a young woman. They are physically out of step with their peers, which often attracts the social attention of older adolescents who assume that the early-maturing adolescent has the interest and capacity and experience to go with his or her more grown-up looks. Adults often jump to the same conclusion.

A young person who physically matures early may face unrealistic expectations from the outside world that he feels compelled to meet. The message these young people get from peers and other adults is "Act as old as you look because that is how we will treat you." So, older boys start showing social interest in your daughter, who is really just in early adolescence but who now feels pressure to grow up fast.

Or consider another hurry factor—social advancement. Suppose that when your athletically gifted fourteen-year-old enters high school, he is encouraged to work out with varsity players. As a freshman, he is suddenly put on the same peer level with seniors. Treated as one of them, your mid-adolescent is routinely exposed to the company of older adolescents and is even invited to their social occasions. Academic acceleration can have the same effect.

If your child experiences an accelerated growth path through adolescence—because of early physical maturity or athletic or academic advancement—the most important component of effective discipline to have in place is open and honest and ongoing communication between the two of you.

Early maturity and social advancement can create pressure to grow up faster. It is unrealistic to expect and demand that a thirteen-year-old who looks seventeen, and who is being treated as a seventeen-year-old by the world, be content to tolerate the limits and restraints of someone four years younger. It is unrealistic to expect and demand that a ninth-grader who hangs out with seniors is going to be content acting like a freshman. It is important, as a conscious parent, to acknowledge the challenges that your child is facing and work with him to find solutions.

Readjusting Expectations

Unless you accept that an adolescent is maturing into an adult, and that this process is a difficult one, you are likely to carry unrealistic expectations into your child's adolescence. These expectations can make parenting a teenager more emotionally difficult than it needs to be.

WHAT YOU'RE USED TO

Expectations are the connections that you create in your mind to anticipate change as you move from an old to a new situation, condition, or relationship. Expectations seek to answer the question "What will the new reality be like?" When your expectations are met, and the new reality is the one that you've anticipated, you tend to feel okay about it, even if you don't like the changes. "Although having a child has changed our marriage, in a lot of ways being parents is working out pretty much how I thought it would." But when the reality is different from what you anticipated, the changes can be difficult to deal with emotionally.

Many "discipline problems" experienced during a child's adolescence are not discipline problems at all, but simply a case of parents' holding on to unrealistic expectations.

There are three kinds of expectations that parents have grown used to their daughter meeting: predictions, ambitions, and conditions. One common prediction is "Our child will follow our rules." When the child meets this prediction, parents feel in control and secure. One common ambition is "We want our child to stay closely connected to family." When the child meets this ambition, parents feel attached and loved. One of their conditions is "Our child should communicate directly and honestly with us." When the child meets this condition, parents feel informed and trustful. In each case, the reality parents expect in their child is the reality they encounter.

CHANGES

When positive expectations of their child are met, parents feel content. But what happens when, in the course of normal developmental change, the adolescent stops behaving exactly like she did as a child, yet parents cling to that old set of expectations? Now there can be an emotional price to pay.

Parents may also feel threatened when their adolescent begins to violate their old conditions and lies to get around their rules to gain more freedom. The child's occasional deceit is not what the parents expected after a childhood in which they could count on the child to deal with them honestly and directly. Now they may feel betrayed, distrustful, angry, or suspicious. When positive expectations are violated, there are usually negative emotional consequences to pay.

EXPECTING EXCEPTIONS

Their child's adolescence is complicated enough for parents without the additional burden of unrealistic expectations. Remember that expectations are not permission. In the previous examples, parents should expect, not necessarily accept, some disobedience, social disconnection, and lying as part of normal adolescence. "Expect" does not mean "accept"!

To expect adolescent changes does not mean you accept them all. "Expect" means to keep your expectations current with the changing reality of your child's growth so you can provide necessary discipline when the unacceptable occurs without overreacting emotionally.

All "expect" means is that you as a parent must anticipate the possibility of these new behaviors in adolescence. Then, when and if they occur, you'll be able to avoid intensifying problems with the child by adding your own emotional difficulties from feeling surprised, disappointed, or betrayed. Instead, because the adolescent's behavior was not unexpected, you can just focus on what the teenager needs to be doing differently—acting more obediently, staying more adequately connected with family, telling the truth.

The Four Stages of Adolescence

To help you understand the normal changes of adolescent growth, what follows is a brief description of the adolescent process, with common problems parents encounter in each of the four stages along the way.

EARLY ADOLESCENCE

Early adolescence usually unfolds between ages nine and thirteen, and problems are characterized by these common changes. The adolescent:

- Develops a negative attitude.

- Shows increased dissatisfaction at being defined and treated as a child.

- Shows less interest in traditional childhood activities and more boredom and restlessness from not knowing what to do.

- Feels a new sense of grievance about unfair demands and limits that adults in life impose.

- Resists authority more, with questioning, arguing, delaying compliance, and ignoring normal home and school responsibilities.

- Experiments more to see what he can get away with, including such activities as shoplifting, vandalizing, prank calls, and the beginning of substance experimentation.

MIDADOLESCENCE

Midadolescence usually unfolds between ages thirteen and fifteen, and problems are characterized by these common changes. The adolescent:

O Fights more with parents over social freedom.

O Lies more often to escape consequences from wrongdoing or to get to do what you have forbidden.

O Feels more peer pressure to go along with risk-taking in order to belong, including more pressure to use illegal substances to be accepted.

LATE ADOLESCENCE

Late adolescence usually unfolds between ages fifteen and eighteen, and problems are characterized by these common changes. The adolescent:

O Gains more independence by doing grown-up activities— part-time employment, driving a car, dating, and recreational substance use at social gatherings.

O Experiences more significant emotional (and often sexual) involvement in romantic relationships.

O Feels grief over the gradual separation from old friends (and perhaps leaving family) and more anxiety at his lack of readiness to undertake more worldly independence.

Maintain realistic expectations about your child's passage through adolescence, and you will reduce the likelihood of overreacting when normal problems occur and helpful disciplinary support is required.

TRIAL INDEPENDENCE

Trial independence usually unfolds between ages eighteen and twenty-three, and problems are characterized by these common changes. The adolescent struggling to be adult:

O Has lower self-esteem from a sense of incompetence, not being able to adequately support all the demands and keep all the commitments of adult responsibility at this "grown-up" age.

O Feels anxious over not having a clear sense of direction in life.

O Is easily distracted by peers who are confused about direction, too, partying more to deny problems or escape responsibility, as the period of maximum exposure to drug and alcohol use begins.

Substance Abuse and Informing Your Child

Like it or not, drugs and alcohol are prevalent in modern society and, at some point, your child is likely to be exposed to them. Whether legal or illegal, recreational or medicinal, and whether found in your bathroom cabinet or in your cleaning closet or garage, dangerous substances exist. The adolescent years are ripe for experimentation with these drugs.

What are you as parents supposed to do? Since you can't change the world, does that mean you are helpless to protect your children from the dangers of alcohol and drugs? No! You can't actually control your child's choices when it comes to alcohol and drug use, but you can definitely inform those choices with the best information and understanding you have. You can inform your child about the nature of the problem, about the risks involved, and about keeping herself safe should she make the decision to use.

SIGNS OF SUBSTANCE USE TO WATCH FOR

It takes parental vigilance to help keep a child drug-free, so parents need to know what signs of substance use to watch for. There are general and specific indicators worth keeping an eye out for as your child makes the journey through adolescence.

Some of the general indicators have to do with your teenager's making decisions that seem uncharacteristic or inconsistent with the established history and true character of the person as you know her to be. In each case, substance use takes the user from a caring to a noncaring (freedom from normal caring) mental frame of reference. Here are some common examples.

- A normally honest child starts lying.

- A normally smart child starts making unwise decisions.

- A normally motivated child starts becoming apathetic.

- A normally well-performing child starts failing.

- A normally obedient child starts getting into social trouble.

- A normally even-tempered child starts becoming explosive.

- A normally confiding child starts avoiding communication.

- A normally responsible child starts acting irresponsibly.

Always be on the lookout for atypical changes in your child as she journeys through adolescence. None of these general changes by themselves are sure signs of substance use, but three or four of them together should cause you to ask whether alcohol or drug use may be disorganizing your teenager's life. Keep in mind that denial is an aspect of addiction. It may seem like your teenager is blatantly lying, but to her, perhaps not. It can be baffling.

There are also specific indicators to be on the lookout for. Here are some common behaviors that could indicate a substance abuse issue:

- You receive phone calls for your child where the caller refuses to give a name or just hangs up.

- You discover empty alcohol containers or drug paraphernalia in her room, backpack, or car.

O Your child is charged with possession, possession with intent to distribute, or driving while intoxicated.

O Money or items are stolen from family members.

O Your child is in possession of more money than you are providing.

O Your liquor supply is disappearing faster than you are drinking it, or it is watered down.

O There is a steady decline in your child's school attendance, a rise in disciplinary problems at school, and more rule breaking at home.

If you see three or four of these indicators present in your child's life and she cannot give you a satisfactory explanation for these behaviors, you may want to take her to a certified substance abuse counselor to assess whether alcohol or drugs are playing a part in what is going on.

COPING WITH TEENAGE SUBSTANCE USE

It's important for the conscious parent to understand that substance abuse is not necessarily an indicator of inappropriate parenting. Accepting that you are not perfect and neither is your child will help you to navigate the waters ahead.

In their fear of the problem, parents often think punishment is the best deterrent to further use. It is not. To persuade yourself of this reality, just consider the high percentage of people in jail for drug or drug-related offenses. They are being punished, but how many of them come out and live drug-free? Not many. The most significant way you can deal with this issue is communication. What might you communicate? Consider the following.

O **State your value position.** "You do not have our blessing to use alcohol or drugs. If you choose to use drugs or alcohol, there will be consequences."

O **Give a rational explanation against use.** "There are a lot of ways you can get hurt as you grow through adolescence. Substance use only increases these risks. We want you to follow a sober path because that is safest."

- **Offer to share your personal and current history with alcohol and drug use.** "I would like to give you the benefit of what alcohol and drug experience I have had so you can learn from what I've learned, from dangers I've seen, and from mistakes I've made. In return, I would like you to share your exposure to substances with me so I can help you learn from the experience."

- **Share any history of substance use problems in the immediate and extended family.** "Here are some cautionary stories about how substance use has caused problems for some of the people in our family system that you know. Perhaps hearing about choices they made can inform choices that you make."

- **Declare the topic of substances and substance use a topic always open for family discussion.** "It is important for us to talk about alcohol and drugs as they indirectly or directly affect your experience—from what you hear, from what you see, and from what you may decide to do. Of course, if you ever have any questions or concerns about my substance use, like alcohol, I'm open to discussing that."

GET HELP

If the warning signs have led to your assessment that your teenager is using alcohol to intentional excess or using other drugs that in a wide variety of ways are creating dangerous risk-taking or causing physical harm, then you must take protective action. When your child shows signs of intentional excess, abuse, or addiction, discussing the situation with him may not be enough. If you have a serious concern, get a qualified drug abuse counselor to assess your teenager's substance use. Be open with your child, and let him know that you are seeking help, and why. The response from your child might not be favorable, but failure to get outside assistance could have life-threatening consequences. It will help confirm or deny your suspicions, it will show your child that you are seriously concerned about the possibility of harmful substance use in her life, and it will open the door to some level of treatment if that is advised. And, at the same time, keep the friendly channels of discussion open. Always be available for a ride home if your child needs it.

Don't enable your substance-abusing teenager by solving her problems, giving her second chances, or rescuing her from consequences. The more you "help" in these ways, the more power of self-help you encourage the child to give up and the more learning from experience you prevent. Attend Al-Anon (*www.alanon.com*) meetings yourself for support and guidance.

What kinds of conditions for healthy and responsible family living do parents typically impose on a child who has been abusing substances? Here are a few.

- There will be zero tolerance for alcohol and drug use.
- There will be random drug testing.
- There will be no discretionary money.
- There will be no driving unless to school and back and to work and back, subject to parental supervision.
- There will be no going to parties and all socializing will be subject to parental approval.
- Any paychecks from employment will be turned over to parents for approved spending, agreed-upon saving, and making restitution for any thefts or damages that substance-using behavior has caused.
- All household rules will be followed and all family activities will require cheerful participation.

As these and other conditions for personal conduct are met, as the teenager shows evidence of living in more constructive, drug-free ways, this good behavior will be rewarded with more freedom and independence. Finally, remember that the surest way to raise "drug-free" children is to be drug-free parents—either using in moderation with no problems in their own or other people's eyes, or simply not using at all.

The Freedom Contract

The entire ten- to twelve-year process of adolescence is fraught with risks. Your child will be trying out many experiences for the first time, he'll be exposed to more worldly influences than ever before, and he will generally be unappreciative of the demands and limits of responsibility that you are striving to teach.

Frustrated by your refusal to grant permission, your adolescent may complain, "You never let me do anything! Everyone else has more freedom than I do! You just don't want me to grow up!" This is why, at the outset of adolescence (by ages nine to ten), you must make it very clear that, when it comes to granting more freedom, you intend to hold your child to the freedom contract.

What do you need from your teenager when he or she wants permission for more freedom from you? You want evidence that your adolescent is trustworthy in five distinct ways. Together they add up to form the "freedom contract," stipulating conditions that your teenager must meet before you agree to risk allowing more discretionary choices. The five provisions are:

1. "You will keep us reasonably informed by giving us adequate and accurate information about what is going on in your life and what you are planning to do."

2. "You will live in a two-way relationship with us, doing for us in fair exchange for our doing for you, contributing to the family as the family contributes to you."

3. "You will honor your word, keeping agreements and following through on commitments you make with us."

4. "Your conduct will be your passport to permission by showing us responsible behavior at home, at school, and out in the world."

5. "You will be available for a free and open discussion of any concern we may need to discuss."

When your teenager wants to negotiate more freedom—such as a later curfew, permission to date, or getting a driver's license—he knows that he must meet these five provisions first. This means demonstrating by actions, not just in words. You are not interested in promises. You are accepting only evidence of performance. Promises have no bargaining power.

If parents want their child to live up to the freedom contract, then they need to honor those five provisions as well. Model the standards of responsibility to which you hold your child.

At such negotiation points, if your teenager has shown evidence of being truthful, being helpful, keeping agreements, acting responsibly, being open to discussion, and talking respectfully, then you tend to be more inclined to consent with his request.

If, however, your teenager has not been living up to the contract (lying to you, taking but not giving, breaking agreements, acting irresponsibly, refusing to discuss concerns with you, or communicating disrespectfully), then you may be inclined to deny the request. You may even reduce existing freedom for a while until the provisions of the freedom contract begin to be honored once again.

Behavior Snapshot

Adolescence is a long process of transformation and separation. Your once compliant child may now be a disinterested, self-centered hormonal creature who thinks you are an impossible warden. But if you know what to expect, then when the changes in your child do occur you won't feel so overwhelmed or emotionally distraught.

What happens: Your teenage daughter tells you that she may be pregnant.

What you *want* to do: Scream at her that she is ruining her life and yours, too.

What you should do: Thank her for confiding in you. Work out some rational actions—make an appointment with a doctor; talk about options for the pregnancy (if there is one); visit a family planning clinic with her if she is afraid to go alone; include all responsible parties in the discussions as decisions are made—your partner, your daughter's partner, the parents of the father of the child (if there is a confirmed pregnancy).

Important Points to Consider

Adolescence is often viewed as a period of emotional turmoil and upheaval. As a conscious parent, you can be there to guide your child through the separation process and influence him to make positive choices.

- There are four stages of adolescence: early adolescence, midadolescence, late adolescence, and trial independence.

- Unfortunately, drugs and alcohol are realities of life, and chances are your child will be exposed to them. Should you suspect that your child has a substance abuse problem, it's important to address the problem and not blame your parenting or express anger against your child.

- Adolescents are not simply large children. As a child reaches adolescence, your expectations must evolve.

- Creating a "freedom contract" will allow your child to experience independence within the confines of your family's structure and expectations.

CHAPTER 16

Constructive Conflict

Disagreement between parent and teenager is one defining (and yes, healthy) feature of adolescence. Yet, an increase in conflicts does not necessarily mean that parent and teenager don't get along. Although you had disagreements over discipline with your child when she was younger, when her adolescence approaches, your child will find even more opportunities for conflict. Your teenager is willing to fight for more independence, the right to individuality, and the need for less parental restraint. She now complains about how your discipline impedes her freedom to grow.

Why Conflict Is Necessary

Conflict is the process of communication through which family members confront and resolve inevitable differences in wants, values, beliefs, perceptions, and goals that arise between them. Because adolescence is the time when your child begins to differentiate herself from the child she once was, from how you are as parents, and from how you want her to be, there are many more differences for parents to deal with during their daughter's teenage years.

No matter how little household help you require, you may be told you are demanding too much. No matter how much oversight you let go, you may be told you are overprotective. No matter how much you try to listen, you may be told you don't understand. No matter how much you explain them, you may be told your rules don't make sense. No matter how much you allow and provide, you may be told that friends are allowed and provided more. No matter how just you try to be, you may be told you are unfair. No matter how informed and up-to-date you try to be, you may be told you are hopelessly out of touch with reality and behind the times. During your child's adolescence, it often seems in her eyes that a "bad" parent is the best parent you can be.

Your willingness to constructively, openly, and respectfully engage in conflict over disciplinary issues, and share your reasons for doing so, for the sake of your teenager's best interests—against what she may want—is a major part of your parental responsibility during adolescence. During the difficult times, remember that your goal is to raise a person who can exist on her own outside the nest.

Having some differences is unavoidable and even healthy, and experiencing some conflict is inevitable, but violence is never the answer. It is up to parents to teach and monitor safety in the conduct of family conflict.

Consider how the potential for conflict is built into family life. There may be conflict over cooperation: Who shares what? There may be conflict over control: Whose way shall prevail? There may be conflict over competition: Who gets most? There may be conflict over conformity: Who goes along with whom?

These kinds of conflicts give rise to common grievances from adolescents.

- **Cooperation:** "Why do I need to help?"

- **Control:** "Why can't I decide for myself?"

- **Competition:** "Why don't we ever do what I want?"

- **Conformity:** "Why do I have to do what the family does?"

The Nature of Conflict

Conflict is not fundamentally about disagreement. It is really about agreement—two parties listening to one another and understanding where the disagreement occurs. When parent and teenager both disagree over chores, curfew, or cleaning up, and then choose to resolve that difference through argument, then conflict occurs. Conflict is a matter of mutual choice.

COOPERATING IN CONFLICT

To put it another way, conflict is always cooperative. It takes two to create a debate. So one formula for conflict is:

Conflict = Resistance versus Resistance

This is a helpful formula to remember when your teenager, after a stressful day at school, is looking for an argument, but you are not. "You never let me do anything!" he begins, inviting you into disagreement. But you choose not to argue in response, so no argument takes place. Instead you offer a different option: "If you've had a hard day, I'd be willing to hear about it." By refusing to engage, and offering to listen, you set limits on how much conflict you are willing to help create. By responding to the underlying feeling, you are being empathetic and sensitive to your child's needs.

Although it can feel natural to fight for what is right every time, you cannot emotionally afford to fight about every difference that arises between you and your teenager. One secret of relationship survival in adolescence is being careful to choose your battles with thought and care. Encourage your child to express her emotions, be mindful about underlying issues, and choose debates with care.

PICKING YOUR BATTLES

For most parents, conflict with their teenager is stressful. It feels frustrating, and frustration can cause anger. Sometimes discomfort with one's own or the other person's anger causes anxiety. In either case, it can have a negative effect on your attitude. In addition, conflict with your teenager can prove to be contagious when, after arguing with their adolescent, parents find themselves bickering with each other.

The most powerful influence on how children engage in conflict is how their parents conduct conflict, so thoughtfully model the approach you want. Your children learn from watching how you disagree with others and with them.

For most teenagers, however, conflict with parents is not a source of extreme stress. It is just fighting for freedom. It even has some positive aspects to it. It can be a chance to express built-up feelings, to test power by challenging authority, and to assert individuality by taking stands for independence. In most cases, the contest is a mismatch, like out-of-shape amateurs (the parents) exchanging blows with a well-conditioned professional (the teenager). So after one of these rounds is over, while parents have a need to lie down and recover from the exertion, their teenager is not even winded, talking on the phone to a friend as if nothing particular has happened. It's okay to accept your exhaustion and allow yourself time to re-group.

Therefore, to conserve energy and moderate stress, parents need to be selective about which differences between themselves and their teenager they wish to actively oppose. If they do not exercise this selective control, they may end up feeling like "battered parents," cooperating in more conflict than is good for them. Parents must remember that conflict with their teenager is a matter of choice.

The Dance of Conflict

Sometimes parents will object to the notion that they have a role in supporting unwanted conflict with their teenager. For example, a single-parent father will describe a ritual conflict that unfolds five days a week with his adolescent daughter, whom he truly believes is responsible for the end-of-day fighting between them. "As soon as she walks in from school, she starts it," he declares. "She won't do as I ask. She won't begin her chores. It's all her fault." But diagramming the interaction tells a somewhat different story.

> Parents who blame their teenager for fighting with them may not be looking at the whole picture. To reduce the fighting, allow yourself to manage your role in each instance of conflict.

As soon as she walks in the door, her father asks her to begin her chores. In response, his daughter complains: "I'm tired. I'll do them later!" Now the father stops asking and demands: "I told you to start your chores now!" In response, his daughter argues: "You never give me a chance to unwind after school. I need some time to relax." Now her father, to show he means business, adds on an additional assignment: "For refusing to do your regular chores, you can have some more to do as well!" In response, his daughter refuses: "That's not fair! There's no way I'll do extra!" Now her father threatens: "If you don't do as you're told, there'll be no going out this weekend!" Now his daughter explodes: "You always punish me when you don't get what you want!" Now her father explodes: "You never do what you're asked!" The fight, which has by now become a ritual of daily life during the week, commences, father and daughter trading angry accusations back and forth to no good effect.

This conflict is so well practiced that it takes less than a minute to fully develop. Then, when both parties run out of angry energy and separate to get relief, the daughter does what she was initially asked. Asked why she went through all that conflict only to end up complying with her father's initial request, she replies, "Because I don't like being pushed around when I get home. He doesn't have to always greet me with a chore right away. He does have different choices, you know!" And she has a right to these feelings. They both could make different choices. He could choose not to immediately ask, demand, add on, and threaten. She can choose not to immediately complain, argue, and refuse. But this sequence has become so automatic on both sides that each feels trapped by the other, totally blames the other, feels helpless and a victim, and so has no way out. Furthermore, there may be underlying issues that spur on the need for this battle.

The way to stop the conflict is not for them to change each other, but to take individual responsibility for the cooperative choices each of them is making. By changing those choices, they can keep the conflict from happening. The first step is to discuss the situation, during a calm moment. Taking the time to hear each other, when the conflict is not as urgent, opens the door for discovery. So, the father might make some changes in his choices based on his daughter's feedback. "When you come home, the first thing I want is to hear how your day was. The second is to give you time to unwind. And the third is to get some help around the house." The daughter could also make some changes in her choices. "When I come home, the first thing I want you to know is that I don't want you to do all the family work yourself. The second is I want a couple of minutes to catch my breath. And the third is I want to start giving you the help I know you need." So now they start to work with each other and not against each other.

Tactics to Avoid

There are two kinds of tactics that teenagers commonly use in conflict: distraction and manipulation. This doesn't mean that your child is "bad," they are simply a mechanism for testing limits. Both tactics undermine the conflict resolution process by getting in the way of honest, open, and direct communication about the issue at hand. Distraction tactics are used to keep from losing. Manipulation tactics are used to "force" a win.

DISTRACTION TACTICS

It's normal to resort to distraction tactics in arguments that one is losing, trying to change the focus to an issue where there is a better chance of winning. Suppose you want to discuss with your twelve-year-old son why he's not turning in his homework, and what needs to change to solve this. You start by dealing with the specific:

"You have not been turning in your homework this week."

Rather than reply to the specific issue for which he has no defense, he tries to shift the topic to an abstract complaint: "The only thing you care about is how I do in school!"

Do not let distraction tactics cause you to get off the disciplinary point you are dedicated to resolve.

But you stick to the issue, restating it with accuracy: "Your teacher told me that the last four days, you have not turned in your homework."

Having no accurate data to counter this charge, he now resorts to using extremes: "You never believe me; you always believe the teacher!"

But you stick to the issue, restating it in the present: "As matters now stand, you are not turning in your homework."

Having no present data to contradict you, he now tries to shift the focus to past and future: "This is just what you do, holding what's already happened against me, refusing to trust that I'll do better next time!"

But you stick to the issue, restating it in terms of responsibility: "It is your job to do your homework and turn it in."

Having no evidence of responsibility to refute you, he tries to shift the focus with blame: "It's the teacher's fault for not making sure I wrote the homework down!"

But you stick to the issue by sticking to the evidence: "You have not been turning in your homework, and, in order to pass, it needs to be done."

Having no evidence to defend with, he resorts to excuses: "Maybe I just forgot; people do forget, you know!"

But you stick to the issue by relentlessly staying on the subject: "You have not been turning in homework and that needs to be done."

Having no facts to dispute your charge, he makes one last attempt to shift the focus by getting you off the subject: "You always get after me about school, but never my sister, because she's your favorite!"

But you are steadfast. You will not be distracted: "I want to discuss with you why homework is not being turned in and what you need to do so."

MANIPULATION TACTICS

A child may resort to manipulation tactics when she wants to overcome a refusal you have made. For example, you have just refused your sixteen-year-old permission to attend a late-night party just outside of town to which some of her friends ("all of them," according to her) have been allowed to go. Unable to persuade you out of your decision with reasonable argument, she turns to emotional manipulation to try to change your mind.

Another name for this manipulation is emotional extortion. Long ago, before acquiring speech, the infant/toddler discovered that strong emotional expression could sometimes change a parental "no" into a "yes."

So, first, your teenager uses an expression of love. "I love you so much, you're the most wonderful parent! You always understand me and what I need!" And feeling flattered in response to this expression of emotion, perhaps you re-evaluate your refusal. But in the end, you still say no.

Now, since declarations of love didn't work, your teenager may turn to anger. "You never let me do anything! I'll never forgive you for not letting me go!" And feeling rejected in response to this expression of emotion, perhaps you re-evaluate your refusal. But in the end, you still say no.

Now since anger didn't work, your teenager may turn to suffering. "You've made me so unhappy! I'll never get over this hurt!" And feeling guilty in response to this tearful expression of emotion, perhaps you re-evaluate your refusal. But in the end, you still say no.

Now since suffering didn't work, your teenager may turn to helplessness. "Oh, what's the point? My life is all up to you anyway. There's nothing I can do!" And feeling pity in response to this expression of emotion, perhaps you re-evaluate your refusal. But in the end, you still say no.

Teach your child to value conflict as a way to safely deepen and strengthen caring relationships in the family. Learning this helps your child to create intimacy around differences in future relationships.

Since helplessness didn't work, your teenager may turn to apathy. "You can decide whatever you want. I don't care what—I don't care about you!" And feeling abandoned in response to this expression of emotion, perhaps you re-evaluate your refusal. But in the end, you still say no.

Now since apathy didn't work, your teenager may turn to threat of injury. "You better watch out! I'll get back at you or maybe I'll even hurt myself!" And feeling scared in response to this expression of emotion, perhaps you re-evaluate your refusal. But in the end, you still say no.

It's doubtful that any teenager will use this full arsenal of emotions on any single occasion to try to overcome parental refusal, but she will often resort to the ones that parents have proven vulnerable to in the past. By adolescence, a child has come to know her parents extremely well, and she's willing to use that knowledge to create the effect she wants. Thus, if you can't stand feeling guilty, expect your teen to express suffering as a manipulation. If you can't stand feeling rejection, expect anger. If you can't stand feeling fear, expect threat. It's important to understand that teenagers are still learning how to interact socially, and parents can serve as a testing ground. Model active listening skills and let your child know when they have said something that you've found hurtful.

Holding your position in the face of this kind of emotional onslaught is not easy, but it is necessary. Emotions should be used to express authentic feelings, not to manipulate people to get one's way in conflict. You want to keep disagreement declarative so differences can be discussed and rationally and empathetically resolved. To this end, you refuse to play emotional extortion with your teenager, and you refrain from using it yourself.

Rules for Family Conflict

Conflict can be dangerous. In war, the outcome (who wins) is more important than the process (any means necessary) because victory is all that counts. In families, the process (how people communicate) is more important than the outcome (the resolution reached) because protecting the future of the relationship is paramount. Adults who "fight to win" encourage unhealthy conflict, rather than healthy debate.

Most acts of family violence and social hate crimes are preceded by name-calling.

In caring relationships, learning to fight well is the work of a lifetime. Being able to confront, discuss, and resolve significant differences without anyone's ever suffering harm takes disciplined conduct. To teach this discipline, it helps to have guidelines and restraints in place to keep conflict constructive.

A few such "rules for family conflict" are listed here.

O **Keep conflict safe.** Conflict is never an acceptable excuse for causing another family member emotional or physical hurt. "Well, I only said that because I was angry" is no excuse. If anger caused anyone to do or say something hurtful, then another way to manage that anger must be found. Any injury received in family conflict should be accidental, never intentional.

O **Have an injury agreement in place in case conflict ever causes, or threatens to cause, physical or emotional harm.** Whenever, in the course of conflict, anyone feels endangered or actually hurt, the issue at difference should immediately be put aside and the hurtful behavior addressed in such a way that it will not occur again. Then conflict over the difference can safely proceed again.

O **Offer all parties the right of separation and a responsibility for return.** Anytime any party in a conflict is getting too worked up emotionally and feels at risk of saying or doing something he might later regret, that person has the right to declare a separation, or a time-out to cool down. At the same time, that person has a responsibility for scheduling a time to return to the discussion when it can be conducted in a more emotionally sober way.

O **Make a commitment to not stop caring.** Particularly for an adolescent, there is a need to know from parents that no matter how hard he pushes against authority in conflict, the teenager is in no danger of pushing their love away.

O **Exercise your right and responsibility to speak up.** All parties are entitled to their say, whether others agree with what they say or not, as long as they don't say it in a disrespectful or abusive manner. They are also responsible for speaking up if they want their desire or opinion known. There is no mind reading. Family members can know only what they are told.

O **Agree to discuss the specifics of your differences in specific terms.** Conflicts cannot be resolved by resorting to abstracts and generalizations. Stick to objective descriptions of happenings and events each side wants or does not want to have occur.

O **Avoid meltdowns.** Conflict creates resemblance, with each party tending to copy influential tactics used by the other. Therefore, parents have to model constructive communication so the teenager is encouraged to imitate their conduct and not the reverse. When parents imitate impulsive adolescent behavior in conflict (voice-raising, interrupting, and insulting), then a meltdown has occurred—now the parents are communicating on the teenager's terms.

O **Do not allow name-calling.** Name-calling, attaching a negative label to the other person in conflict, is like loading a gun. The bad name can be used to justify bad treatment. "If you're going to act like a crybaby, then I'll really give you something to cry about!"

○ **Avoid making extreme statements.** It is easy to trade "You always" and "You never" accusations, both of which distort the other person's record. "On this occasion" is closer to the truth.

○ **Do not carry over emotion or issues from one conflict to the next.** There are no carryovers. No unfinished grievance left over from a previous conflict can become activated in the next, and there should be no anxiety about the next conflict based on how the last one was conducted. Any attempted carryover of either kind needs to be addressed, or your next conflict will be harder to resolve.

○ **Remember that the goal in family conflict is intimacy.** There are two ways to get intimacy in relationships—by sharing human similarities and by confronting differences. The goal of conflict is to safely confront differences, talking them through to reach a settlement that both parties can live with, each coming to better know the other and feel better known by the other than was the case before, their relationship strengthened by the understanding and agreement between them.

Behavior Snapshot

Conflict with your teenager can seem to be a way of life. But it takes two people to enter into a conflict, and you can make the mental choice not to get into an altercation with your teen. Of course your teen may try to manipulate or distract you in her relentless determination to get her way, but you are too smart to fall into this trap. You know that by staying on track and addressing the problem, you can minimize the conflicts with your teen and solve problems without anyone becoming seriously hurt.

What happens: Your teenage daughter has received a generous check from a grandparent for her birthday. Usually in your family, birthday money is spent however the recipient wants to spend it. Your daughter has decided to get a large tattoo with her boyfriend's name covering her forearm. When you object, your daughter engages in verbally aggressive conflict.

What you *want* to do: Take away her money until she regains her senses. Argue your point by telling her that she is wrong and has no right to use her money this way. Change the family custom of letting her decide how she wants to spend her birthday money. Punish her for making the suggestion.

What you should do: Loosen the reins a little bit, and be a part of the process of helping her make a decision that could have a major impact on her life. Rather than engaging in an "I'm right, you're wrong" argument, listen to your daughter's reasoning for wanting the tattoo. Does she believe it will please her boyfriend or impress her friends? Understand that she may not fully understand or be able to express these reasons. Share your concerns about judgment she may be subject to because of a visible tattoo. Model thoughtful behavior by offering alternatives. If she waits six months before moving ahead, you will revisit the subject and accompany her if she chooses to move forward.

Important Points to Consider

Conflict within the parent-child relationship is normal, and a certain level of conflict is even healthy. There are certain measures that you can take to ensure that conflict with your child will result in a well-functioning adult.

- Pleading or demanding for consent shifts the power in a relationship. Allowing children to make appropriate choices encourages mutual respect.

- Lack of compliance can lead to high frustration levels. It's okay to take a time-out and allow yourself to accept your anger and deal with it.

- Providing choices enhances a child's ability to make good decisions, even when you're not around.

 **CHAPTER 17**

Early Adolescence (Ages Nine to Thirteen)

It takes courage for your child to begin the process of adolescence, pushing against and pulling away from your control to gain more independence from family and freedom for self-determination, letting his independent side out, arousing some degree of your disapproval in the process. It also takes courage for you to parent your child through adolescence, embracing change and new processes. You can successfully traverse this difficult part of life by closely following conscious parenting techniques.

Signs of Early Adolescence

The onset of adolescence opens a new chapter in your parenting life. Now you face the challenge of keeping up loving closeness and discipline with your son as more social separation and conflict over differences are helping you to start growing apart. Although parents commonly identify adolescence with the "teenage" years, early adolescence actually begins well before that, usually unfolding between the ages of nine and thirteen.

The second-grade teacher may describe most of the class as usually serious, focused, calm, good-humored, curious, industrious, attentive, enthusiastic, positive, cooperative, and friendly; the fifth-grade teacher may describe most of the class as often silly, disorganized, restless, moody, disinterested, indolent, distracted, apathetic, negative, resistant, and even hostile. As you can see, changes in behavior are quite common. Your son might not only be more difficult to parent, but also be more difficult to teach. You're not the only adult who is contending with this transformation. And your child is not the only one growing through this change.

A sure sign that your child has entered adolescence is when you have become a social embarrassment to your son in public. The first-grader responds to your surprise classroom visit with delight, but the same surprise generally mortifies your fifth-grader.

YOUR CHILD'S CHANGING BEHAVIOR

Even if you had unquestioned authority in childhood, you will likely experience questioned authority in early adolescence. If you were your child's preferred company before, you will come second to the company of his friends now. If you were the object of appreciation before, you will receive more complaints and criticism now. Parents who take these changes personally and feel disrespected, rejected, or otherwise devalued often want to pull away or even be negative in return. "Well, if that's the way you're going to act, I don't want anything to do with you!" This is a mistake.

From here on out, your child needs you more than ever for the consistency of your caring, for the influence of your communication, and for the stability of your support. Thus, if you are a parent who had a "best friend" relationship with your child, always confiding in each other and doing things together, and now has an early adolescent who wants to talk less and disclose less to you than before, don't cut off conversation or invitations to companionship. Keep initiating opportunities to talk; keep the door open to communication so your child has a continuing chance to talk with you when he feels willing and able. Keep asking your child to do things with you, and don't let refusals keep you from continuing to extend these invitations. Don't treat normal adolescent separation as rejection.

Do not grow out of "touch," literally, with your adolescent. Feeling too grown-up to accept being hugged and kissed by you, your early adolescent will still accept a friendly pat on the shoulder that physically expresses your loving care.

SIGNS OF CLOSENESS

Remember, separating from childhood is also painful for your son. He doesn't want to be treated and defined as a child anymore, but he still misses a lot of the closeness that was a part of those early years. For example, no longer willing to snuggle up or be kissed because he feels too grown-up for these old shows of affection, your eleven-year-old allows (and needs) a sideways hug and an "I love you," both of which he can still accept. To be treated "as a child" feels embarrassing; but to be denied all expressions of parental affection that went with "being a child" feels isolating.

Understanding Insecurity and Low Self-Esteem

Change is scary for your early adolescent, knowing she is transforming, but to what effect? Consider some of the levels on which your child is beginning to change.

PHYSICAL CHANGES

Physically there is the feeling of being helpless over one's body, particularly if puberty has started to release estrogen and testosterone. Now the child becomes self-conscious about body hair and body odor, the girl contending with growing breasts and menstruation, the boy seeing his testicles enlarge and having wet dreams, both children careening through growth spurts over which they have no power. And if puberty has not begun for them but has for others, that becomes cause for concern. "When will I start looking more grown up?" Each morning there is the excruciating encounter with the mirror, examining oneself pore by pore to see what awful change has befallen one's body overnight that must be taken to school for everyone to see, for everyone to make fun of. "Look at her!" "Look at him!"

The early adolescent truly believes that other people will be as merciless in their scrutiny as the adolescent is with herself. So, the adolescent explodes in anger at her parents, who are trying to be reassuring about her appearance: "Don't tell me I look nice. I know how awful I look!"

Personal insecurity created by developmental change can cause early adolescents to engage in social cruelty by ganging up. A social bully intimidates a social victim, with followers collaborating in mistreatment that they fear receiving themselves.

EMOTIONAL AND SOCIAL CHANGES

The early adolescent lives in fear of, and fascination with, the harsh and violent side of the outside world she is about to begin exploring. Then there are intense mood swings, with more extreme lows than highs, which seem unpredictable and inexplicable.

Socially, the world of peers (most of whom are beset by similar insecurity) has become extremely competitive, conniving, and cruel, as friends vie with each other for group membership and popularity. Relationships become extremely unstable. Yesterday's best friend may not speak to your child tomorrow. Rumoring and gossip, teasing and bullying, rejecting and excluding are all part of the social harshness of the age. "How do I fit in; who are my real friends?"

Academically, concentration on schoolwork is broken by concern over all these other developmental changes. It's hard to keep one's mind on studying when it feels like one's physical, emotional, and daily social survival are at stake. "It's much harder to do well in school than it was before!"

Beset by personal doubt and the delusion of uniqueness, your child at this age makes an unhappy comparison: "No one else feels the way I do!" She then proceeds to the question that most early adolescents wonder at some point: "What's the matter with me?" The answer is usually a list of indictments provided by her worst fears: "I'm stupid, I'm ugly, I'm a loser, I have no friends."

YOUR APPROACH TO DISCIPLINE

It is worthwhile for you to keep this portrait of early adolescence in mind when it comes to disciplining your child at this very vulnerable age. In general, nonevaluative correction needs to be the order of the day. "We disagree with the choice you have made, this is why, and here is what you need to do in consequence." No personal criticism allowed. Your early adolescent is already too down on herself for her own good.

Most importantly, do not put your early adolescent down with teasing, humor, or sarcasm. Being laughed at, being made fun of, being ridiculed, and being made to look foolish all lead to the most painful emotional state at this age: embarrassment. And although embarrassment may seem a slight discomfort for you, it is one small step from shame for the early adolescent. Children take special handling at this painfully self-conscious and insecure age. You don't want to make a hard passage worse.

If your early adolescent has a teacher who uses public putdowns to keep students in their place, meet with the teacher to affirm your support for classroom order and to express concern about the use of sarcasm as a classroom management technique.

Separation from Childhood

Early adolescence begins the separation from childhood. This unique person, through words and actions, begins to differentiate himself from the child he used to be. This differentiation is commonly expressed in three ways.

○ "I am different from how I was as a child," your son seems to say, and now rejects much of what used to be valued, while trying on new images, interests, activities, and associations.

○ "I want to be treated differently than I was as a child," your son seems to say, and now demands fewer traditional restraints and more independent freedom.

○ "I am becoming different from how you are," your son seems to say, and now develops new cultural tastes and identifications that are counter to those you have traditionally held, and that fit less well into the family.

INCREASED RESISTANCE

Each type of "different" statement, each time it is made, is a statement of separation. And when you have reached your tolerance limit for this differentiation and draw the line ("I will not allow that kind of poster on your bedroom walls!"), your child will, at the least, show resentment and will most likely raise conflict over it. From now on, you will be parenting against more resistance as your early adolescent pushes to create more room to grow. Your son will feel that he fits less well into the family than in his childhood. To some degree, parents and early adolescent will both become more uncomfortable with each other as differentiation occurs.

You are both redrawing the boundaries of definition, which will result in some degree of compromise between you. Your early adolescent will not get freedom to act as completely different as he would like, and you will come to tolerate more different behavior in your son than you ever thought you would.

MORE CORRECTIVE DISCIPLINE

In this process of separation, particularly if your son was mostly on good behavior in childhood, it can feel that he is now letting his "bad side" out. "Bad" doesn't mean evil, immoral, or unlawful. It means becoming more resistant, oppositional, and abrasive to live with.

Teenagers are naturally offensive. A healthy teenager pushes for maximum freedom to grow as soon as he can get it. Healthy parents restrain that push out of concerns for safety and responsibility. This is the healthy conflict of opposing interests that unfolds over the course of adolescence.

In response, parents usually become more corrective in order to keep the early adolescent in line. By becoming more corrective, parents are now seen as not as "nice" to live with, and seem "meaner." This is a necessary change in the relationship. For a child to justify early adolescent changes that go with letting the bad side out, it helps if he sees parents as letting their bad (corrective) side out, too. "If you can be harder to live with," the early adolescent seems to say, "then so can I."

A SIGN IT'S WORKING

There is, however, one critical distinction you want your son at this age to be able to make. You'll know your child has made this distinction when your adult friends compliment you on how well-behaved your early adolescent is in their presence. "You can't be describing our child!" you protest, knowing how difficult your relationship with him at home can sometimes be. But the eyes of the world don't lie. Your early adolescent has enough common social sense to understand not to treat outside adults the way he sometimes treats you. What is the motivation behind this behavior? What is your child attempting to communicate to you?

Your child is doing what you want him to: showing his good side out in the world and letting his bad side out only with you at home, reserving it for the adults whom he trusts to keep loving him no matter how resistant his behavior. Since every adolescent needs room to express both good side and bad, you'd rather the bad was confined to home while the good was shown to the outside world.

The Negative Attitude

One of the first signs of early adolescence is what parents often describe as "the bad attitude." It often comes out of nowhere. Here is a child who used to be so positive about life, so enthusiastic, and now it's as if someone has pulled the plug and all that positive energy has been drained away. Now the child just lies around, frustrated and bored and restless, complaining about having "nothing to do." But no matter what suggestion you make for an activity, you are told that your idea is a bad one and that you just don't understand. So then you decide that since your child doesn't know what to do, and there is plenty of work to be done around the place, maybe what you need to do is ask her to do some work. "Not now! Leave me alone! Can't you see I'm tired?" comes the offended response. Then the phone rings, and suddenly there's plenty of energy to go hang out with a friend.

Now negative energy begins to build. As a child, your daughter probably accepted that her personal freedom depended on your permission, and more often than not, that was okay with her. Now, however, with childhood closing down and the exciting grown-up world opening up, your limits and demands are becoming a major grievance. "What do you mean you won't let me? That's not fair! Who gave you the right to tell me what I can and can't do? You're not the boss of the world!" But you are the boss of the early adolescent's world, and now she doesn't like it. It is this negativity, caused by the loss of old enthusiasms and the onset of new grievances, that creates the negative attitude.

The negative attitude begins the process of adolescence. People do not want to personally change unless they are dissatisfied with who and how they are. Now the early adolescent wants a change. She doesn't want to be defined and treated as a "child" anymore. Early adolescence can coincide with the onset of puberty, but it doesn't have to. When it does, early adolescence is considerably more intense. But the primary motivator in early adolescence is the dissatisfaction generated by the negative attitude.

Two common disciplinary problems created for parents at the negative attitude phase of early adolescence are taking negativity out on others and throwing away childish things.

TAKING NEGATIVITY OUT ON OTHERS

No wonder your early adolescent feels negative. She's rejecting the idea of being a child and the interests and attachments that went with it, and doesn't yet have anything positive to replace the loss, so her self-esteem drops. So, after a socially difficult day at school, your eleven-year-old comes home brimming with negativity, immediately picking on a younger brother or sister, driving the child to tears, just to take out bad feelings on someone else. Now negativity about self has turned into meanness toward others, just as it does in peer relationships at school at this age.

Because the early adolescent wants more independence but still wants to be taken care of, parents can get mixed messages at this confused and confusing age. "Leave me alone; keep me company." "Let me do it; do it for me." "Don't make me come; don't leave me behind."

Trying to feel better by trying to make others feel worse, however, is not an acceptable way for your early adolescent to manage negativity. Therefore, you need to confront, discourage, and redirect this behavior. "It is perfectly all right for you to get down about your life, but it is not okay to act those unhappy feelings out on others. Please know that whenever you have a down mood or a bad day, I am always willing to listen, and to help you find a way to feel better if that is what you'd like."

THROWING AWAY CHILDISH THINGS

In the spirit of rejecting the childish part of herself to declare independence from childhood, your early adolescent may want to quit an activity that has historically been an important source of self-esteem. Since you want your daughter to have as many pillars of self-esteem as possible, to give one up at this fragile time does not seem like a good idea. Rather than get into an argument about whose activity it is, however, and who should have the right to make the decision, be willing to consider quitting on the condition that she agrees to a delay. "Let's both think about it for three months. If at the end of that time you still want to give up the sport, we will talk seriously about it. In the meantime, think about all the ways you have enjoyed it—from the pleasure of playing to the company of friends."

During this transition, you may have to put up with a hard compromise. Every practice, your daughter complains about going; you insist, there is an argument, you still insist; she grudgingly gives consent, and once at practice she has a good time. This is the compromise: she gets to protest going there, you get blamed for causing a "childish" activity to be continued, and the early adolescent is then free to continue an old activity that can still be enjoyed because you "made" her go.

Finally, at the end of the period you've agreed on, if your daughter still wants to give up the activity, then agree by imposing another condition. "If you really want to give up this activity, that is okay with me as long as you substitute a similar activity we both agree on in its place. If you do not choose a new activity, you will continue participating in the current one." You want a new support of self-esteem to replace the old.

Recognizing Rebellion

People do not rebel without a reason, and the early adolescent finds just cause for rebellion: what he sees as the infringement of personal freedom. It feels unfair to be made to do what he doesn't want to do, and to be kept from doing what he does want to do. Basic rights of self-determination are being denied by the powers that be at home, at school, and out in the world. What is the early adolescent to do?

The answer is to rebel. Actively and passively, your son becomes more resistant to your demands and restraints, creating two common disciplinary problems for you to deal with—automatic arguments and endless delays.

AUTOMATIC ARGUMENTS

A negative attitude gives the adolescent the motivation to change, and rebellion gives him the power to change. Standing up to parental authority by questioning their demands is one way this is done. Parents who have a low tolerance for argument are often at high risk of overreacting when arguments occur. "Don't you talk back to me!"

Rather than empowering the early adolescent when he attempts to argue with you, remember that it takes two to make an argument. Your son can't argue with you unless you agree to argue back. So when your request is greeted with a challenge back—"Why should I have to do what you say?"—declare your unwillingness to argue and repeat your insistence on what you have asked. "As I said, this is what I need to have you do."

> Because standing up to parents by arguing takes courage, never purposely or nervously smile or laugh during this exchange. Your adolescent may feel ridiculed and humiliated and will get very angry at you for taking lightly what he means seriously and is brave to do.

Before you write off all arguments as being irritating and unproductive, appreciate the plus side of what your son is doing. He is daring to speak up to your authority, is learning how to state his position, is willing to argue his case against more skilled opposition, is secure enough to brave your disapproval, and is tough enough to refuse you automatic or immediate obedience. A child who is willing to stand up to parents is usually willing to stand up to peers and the pressure to conform that they can create. A child who automatically does what his parents ask without any resistance often may be at higher risk of doing what he is told by dominating friends (not to mention dangerous strangers).

ENDLESS DELAYS

So you have asked your early adolescent one, two, three, four times to do the dishes and they are still not done. Every time you agree to "wait a minute," you end up waiting another twenty. So finally, in exasperation, you raise your voice and command, "I want them done now!" Whereupon your son looks at you and in a disapproving voice declares, "Well, you don't have to get so upset about it!" The dishes finally get washed, but not with soap. So you are back to square one.

What's going on? Passive resistance is the power of delay. It's a compromise. In actions, the early adolescent is saying "You can tell me what, I'll tell you when, and when I get enough 'when,' I'll do what you want—partly." The best way to deal with endless delay is with relentless insistence (supervision), or waiting until the next exchange point to get your request met.

Do not give additional power to this passive resistance by getting upset, by backing off your request, or (worst of all) by fulfilling the request yourself. If it's worth asking your child to do, then it is definitely worth not defaulting on your request and doing it yourself. Not only will you let your son win with passive resistance, but you will end up feeling angry at doing what someone else should have done.

Both active and passive resistance work to some degree. The early adolescent does gain more power of self-determination than he had before because no parents can hold out against this resistance all the time. It's the end of the day. You're just human. You're tired. You don't want an argument, you're too weary to pursue delay, so you just let some of your requests go. And every time you do, your son gathers a little more power, which sets the stage for the last phase of early adolescence—early experimentation.

Early Experimentation

With freedom gained from both active and passive resistance, your daughter is now curious to experience the world beyond childhood and to see what illicit freedoms she can get away with. For your early adolescent, this is an exciting proposition. "What if I tried something scary to see what it was like?" You want to prevent the risks your daughter wants to take. Where she sees the possibility for adventure, you see the potential for harm.

But when, for example, you share your concerns about the dangers of experimenting with substances at this age (a time when trying cigarettes and inhalants often begins), your early adolescent either denies any interest or denies that it can cause the harm you say it can. "I've got friends who do it some, and they say they don't get hurt."

Remember, you're not out to change your child's mind; you're out to add your own, more mature, perspective.

When it comes to a lot of early substance experimentation, you can't actually control your child's choice, but you can definitely inform it, and you should. Weigh in with an adult perspective to counter the untruths that your child's peers are all too willing to share. "Your aunt, my sister, smoked cigarettes and got lung cancer. So when your friends tell you smoking is safe, you need to know they are mistaken."

All growth requires taking risks, and all risk-taking is enabled by denial: "Bad things won't happen to me because I'm too smart and I'll be careful." What is frustrating for parents is trying to argue with this denial. So don't do it. Denial is part of this experimental age. Accept it. And then feel free to speak up with all of your concerns about various kinds of risk-taking so your daughter can incorporate what you have to say into what she decides to think.

Early experimentation is about gathering the experience needed to change. To this end, your adolescent's interest in seeing what she can get away with can cause a major set of discipline problems, all involving testing limits, at this time.

TESTING LIMITS

Testing limits should be treated seriously and not discounted by parents who just chalk it up to "innocent mischief." If you don't take your stands for acceptable behavior early, it may soon prove too late.

Three common kinds of limit-testing behavior at this age include prank calling, vandalizing, and shoplifting. In each case, your early adolescent, usually in the company of friends, victimizes someone. When she and her friends make a threatening late-night prank call to the old man down the block, they think it's fun to hear his frightened response. When they spray-paint the outside of the school, they think it's cool to leave their mark on a public place. When they take items from a store, they think they've beaten the system by getting goods for free.

In each case, they're testing social limits to see if they are real, to see if they will hold. As parents, your job is to show your daughter that when you break a social limit and are caught, you pay a social price. Your job is to close the loop of responsibility on these occasions.

CLOSING THE LOOP OF RESPONSIBILITY

For every major violation, a consequence will follow—that's the law of enforcement parents have to mandate at this early experimental age. Confrontation with the victim, responding to the victim, and restitution to the victim must all occur. Of these consequences, the first is the one your daughter will dread the most. She has to face the old man she prank-called and listen to him tell what it felt like to receive a threatening call. She has to face the principal and listen as she describes what it is like to have the school defaced. She has to face the store manager and listen to him say what it was like to be stolen from. This is how the loop of responsibility begins to be closed.

Next, she has to respond to what she has heard in a way that recognizes the hurt that she has inflicted. And finally, some form of restitution to the injured party must be made. By connecting bad choice with unwelcome consequence, parents encourage the early adolescent to rethink testing limits and learn a lesson of responsibility from her misdeed.

Behavior Snapshot

Early adolescence is a difficult time for both parents and their children. It takes a lot of patience and understanding to parent an early adolescent.

What happens: Your young teenage daughter screams from her bathroom early in the morning on a school day. It sounds as if someone was murdered. You have to go to work and do not welcome a crisis.

What you *want* to do: Ignore your teenager and insist that she hurry up.

What you should do: Take a deep breath and ask what is wrong. It's a new zit. Acknowledge that this is a monumental crisis to your self-conscious youngster. Offer her some concealer and go on about your morning preparations.

Important Points to Consider

Early adolescence is a period of tremendous growth and tremendous turmoil. A little bit of understanding can go a long way during this tumultuous time.

- Early adolescence usually starts well before the teenage years begin.

- It is normal and acceptable for a child's behavior to change at the onset of early adolescence.

- Nonevaluative correction is a particularly effective form of discipline during the early adolescent years.

- Though testing limits is common, engaging in activities that harm another's body or self-esteem should never be tolerated.

CHAPTER 18

Midadolescence (Ages Thirteen to Fifteen)

The stage of adolescence where maximum conflict between parents and teenager is likely to occur is midadolescence. At this age, disagreement over freedom is no longer about a theoretical matter of principle, as it was in early adolescence. It has become intensely practical. The teenager begins to contest to what degree you can actually restrict the freedom she wants. "You can't make me, and you can't stop me! You're running a home, not a prison, you know!" Remember, the best approach to parenting in midadolescence is to stay calm, firm, and supportive.

Your Adolescent's Worldview

When your teenager says something like "You can't stop me," of course, on one level, she is correct, but on another, she's running a bluff. You may not have direct control over her choices, but you have plenty of indirect influence: her attachment to you, your persuasive techniques, the importance of your approval, the power of your authority, and her dependence on you in a host of material ways. It may seem tricky, but you will need to strike a balance between her need for your approval and her need to be free of you.

THE PUSH FOR FREEDOM

The push for freedom at this age can be extremely strong, driven by your teenager's frantic need to be out in the world, in the company of friends, doing what they want to do. "If I can't be with them, I won't belong!" It feels as if there is no time but the present, and the teenager will mortgage the future to free up the present by promising anything later for freedom now. "I'll stay home the whole next month if I can just go to the party tonight!"

Conflicts over timing plague the relationship between parents and midadolescents. The teenager feels like she will "die," feels like her life will be "ruined," if you refuse her the freedom that her friends are allowed.

> When you are having doubts about consenting to a request from your midadolescent for more freedom, it's perfectly acceptable to ask for time to think it through. Question for information, check the arrangements, push to get your demands for safety met, and say no if you don't feel comfortable saying yes.

THE TYRANNY OF NOW

Now is very important to the midadolescent, whereas parents are trying to slow down by considering how pleasure now might lead to risks or problems later. To this end, parents want time to think—to gather more information, assess risks, consider safety, and require assurances.

Although the teenager doesn't mind delaying on parental requests, having parents delay on a teenager's request feels intolerable to her. So as parents, you have to hang tough: "If you are saying you have to know right now whether you can go and it's now or never, then our answer is 'never,' because you have to give us time to think through your request."

SOCIAL EXTORTION

So now the teenager ups the pressure on the next request by adding social extortion to the urgency of getting a decision now. In front of a group of impatiently waiting friends, who apparently have already received parental permission, your teenager asks if she, too, can go. Your teenager is banking on your saying yes to spare her the social embarrassment of refusing her request in front of her friends.

Instead, you say that you and she will have to talk about this alone in the next room, and her friends can either wait for your decision or go without her. Now your teenager is embarrassed. "How could you treat me like that, like a little child, with all of them standing there?" Then you explain, "I won't be pressured or trapped into making any quick decisions by being put on the spot in front of your friends."

THE GAME OF LOOPHOLES

To get desired freedom, the midadolescent will often become deceptive. She may play a constant game of looking for loopholes, looking for running room where no parental rule or prohibition has been put into place. After the fact, parents find themselves plugging openings the best they can.

Taking a strong stance against your teenager's stronger wants for social freedom during midadolescence will create more conflict during this typically stormy time. When conflict occurs, be sure to model, and insist on, the quality of communication you want in return.

"Well, you never said I couldn't!" innocently protests the teenager as though she didn't know "borrowing" your credit card was against any rules and considered wrong. Catching up with the unforeseen infraction, the parent replies, "Because I never thought you would! But since you have, you need to know that borrowing without permission is stealing. You can't do that in this family, and you will pay me back!"

Relationship Strains and Maintaining a Positive Perspective

The negative attitude, rebellion, and early experimentation of early adolescence can take a psychological toll on the relationship between you and your son. The old parent/child relationship has been transformed in some predictable ways. The closeness you used to feel has given way to more distance. There are more disagreements to bridge than there used to be. You feel more dissatisfied with each other, former contentment giving way to more criticism on both sides.

By midadolescence, parent and teenager may have a more disaffected relationship. Each side develops a list of common complaints against the other. Parents will often charge, "You're too young to understand. You're too adventurous, too untrustworthy, too uncommunicative, too unhelpful, too messy, too irritating, too unconcerned with family, too unreliable, and too interested in bad music." Teenagers will often charge in return, "Well, you're too old to understand, too protective, too untrusting, too prying, too demanding, too fussy, too easily upset, too concerned with family, too controlling, and too ignorant of good music."

Under no circumstances should you tell your teenager that he is "only going through a phase." This is a dismissive statement. It is insulting. You wouldn't tell someone struggling with the infirmities of aging that he is "only going through a phase."

When these complaints rule the relationship, a healthy mutual dislike can sometimes develop between the parents, who won't stop insisting on responsibility, and the teenager, who won't stop pushing for freedom. To keep this dislike from becoming unhealthy, keep a larger positive perspective and do not use hurtful language or say hurtful things.

Can you remember what it was like to be at this age? Did you sneak around, argue with your parents, or even defy them? Those memories can help you feel some empathy for the angst of your midadolescent child.

Connecting Through the Shell of Self-Centeredness

Midadolescence tends to encapsulate the teenager in three major concerns—with self, with fun, and with now. There is nothing wrong with any of these preoccupations. However, as conscious parents, you don't want these to be the sole concerns that govern your teen's behavior. Just because this shell of self-centeredness is normal at this age doesn't make it okay. To let it go unchallenged would do a disservice to you and your teenager.

Your job is to try to penetrate this shell of self-centeredness with a disciplinary response, training your teenager to focus on additional concerns as well. To this end, in words and actions, you communicate as follows.

- "It's fine to focus on yourself, but you also have to think of others and consider their needs."

- "It's fine to want to have fun, but sometimes you have to work before you have fun or instead of having fun."

- "It's fine to want what you want right now, but sometimes you have to delay gratification or even do without."

During the midadolescent passage, you are responsible for helping your child learn this healthy mix—of self and other, of fun and work, of now and later—so she can put it into practice with others when away from home.

Modeling Responsibility When Your Child Avoids It

At some point in midadolescence, most teenagers will choose to break the rules for freedom's sake, and when they get caught, they will try to escape responsibility for whatever they have done. They fear being held accountable for doing wrong and, as a consequence, having to pay the worst price of all—giving up some precious freedom to pay for what they've done.

When confronted by parents about this misconduct, the teenager typically resorts to four defenses against admitting responsibility.

- **He may lie to get out of trouble:** "The teacher was mistaken. It was another student, not me."

- **He may blame others:** "She drove away without paying; I was just a passenger."

- **He may make excuses:** "I was so tired from staying up late and studying for exams, I just wasn't thinking clearly about what I was doing."

- **He may deny anything happened:** "I don't know what you're talking about!"

When your teenager tries to use these escapes from responsibility, you must hold him accountable for owning the decisions he made and the consequences that followed.

Getting your teenager to engage in a conversation can be tricky. Asking questions can discourage your teen from communication, because now questions are emblematic of authority and invasive of privacy. Instead, model the sharing you want by sharing about yourself, and be accessible anytime he "feels like" talking.

You expect your adolescent to admit the truth and take ownership of his actions. You want to close the loop of responsibility for the present violation, and even more important, you want to provide training for the future. It's important to remember that, even during the tumultuous midadolescent years, your child is viewing you as a model. How do you react to adversity? Do you operate in the now?

The Battle Against Authority

At a time when your teenager acts like your imposition of family demands, rules, and restraints is unwanted, unneeded, oppressive, and intolerable, you must keep that family structure firmly in place for her well-being and protection. At this age your teenager is excited and frightened by the same understanding about personal freedom: "You can't make me and you can't stop me!"

Although your teenager is correct, and although she argues the point at every opportunity, you will mostly be given consent because there is security in the structure you provide, and your daughter knows that. "But is it worth all the conflict?" some weary parents ask. The answer is definitely yes. Your midadolescent needs to push against you to save face in order to go along with you to keep safe. You'll need to be the enemy for a while. It's the nature of this phase of growing individuation.

Understanding the combative nature of the consent you are often given at this age, you typically enforce structure in three ways.

O You make demands. ("This is what you need to do.")

O You set limits. ("This is what you can't do.")

O You allow or apply consequences. ("Because you did that, you must now do this.")

Communicating with Your Teen

Because the midadolescent is preoccupied with personal wants, social friendships, and worldly freedoms, it becomes significantly harder for parents to get the teenager's attention than it used to be. Parents must be persistent with their message, and when the message does get through, it is often not well received. Protective busyness ("Not now, I'm on the phone!"), protective unavailability ("Not now, I've got a friend over!"), and protective belligerence ("Not now, I'm in a bad mood!") all conspire to give parents the same forbidding message: "Leave me alone!" If parents wait until a "good time" to raise a concern or communicate a need, they will never get their say. During midadolescence, even at the "best times" they are likely to be given a hard time for intruding into the teenager's life with an unwanted discussion.

If your teenager complains that you don't understand because the world is different from when you were growing up, agree. Then say, "If you truly want me to understand how life is for young people today, then educate me, tell me about it. I want to learn."

The Power of Peers

In midadolescence a peer group can become a second family of the utmost importance. The more separated from, or opposed to, family a teenager grows, the more attached to friends he becomes. (Family changes such as divorce and remarriage often increase teenage dependence on peers.) Through shared experience and adventure, through support and sympathy, peers are there for each other. They provide what parents cannot—companionship in quest of worldly experimentation and social independence.

BELONGING

Belonging to a peer group, however, comes at a price. To gain and maintain membership in good standing, the teenager must make certain sacrifices.

- A certain amount of individual freedom is given up because conformity is the price of acceptance. "You have to behave like us, believe like us, look like us, like us best, and not do better than us."

- A certain amount of personal honesty is given up. "You have to pretend to enjoy whatever the group decides to do."

- A certain amount of control is given up. "You have to go along with the group to prove you belong."

There is no such thing as a peer group that does not exert peer pressure. However, no group can pressure your teenager into doing anything without his permission. Instilling confidence and encouraging your child to feel good about making positive choices can help him follow the right path when the time comes.

RESISTING PEER PRESSURE

Tell your teenager to try to delay when he feels pressure to do what he doesn't want to do. The more he can delay, the more time he buys to think his way out of the situation. So he can say, "I don't feel like doing that right now." And if his peers get on him for refusing, he can respond by saying, "I didn't say not ever, I said not now. And I don't like being pushed around! Not by anyone!"

Teenagers have a lot of trouble saying no to peers, even though saying no to parents is very easy. This is because refusal won't drive away parental love, but it may well jeopardize standing with peers.

Or he may propose doing something else first. "I'm hungry. I want to get something to eat before we do that." Or he can say he needs to use the bathroom, taking time alone to gather time to think. Delay often works because group ideas tend to be ruled by impulse, so that what everyone was thinking of doing before he went to the bathroom may have changed direction by the time he comes out. Finally, you can also give him permission to use you as an excuse. "I'd like to try some of that stuff, but it's not worth it. My parents test me for drugs, and if I ever show up positive, they'll never let me drive a car."

Finally, not all peer pressure leads young people astray. It can also offer protection. Friends do look out for friends, often keeping them out of trouble. Not all peer pressure is bad. When your teenager states "We take care of each other," he is often telling the truth.

A sense of belonging is a legitimate adult need. Psychologist Abraham Maslow names belongingness as one of the important human needs, coming after food, clothing, and shelter. Your teenager gets some of that need satisfied at home, but as he presses for more separation from the family, he will seek that belongingness elsewhere. This is normal and healthy.

Adolescent Lies

When your daughter enters midadolescence and begins pushing harder for freedom, you may wonder, "Whatever happened to the truth?" She seems more prone to lie both by commission (telling a deliberate falsehood) and by omission (not voluntarily disclosing all that parents need to know).

You should consistently communicate where you stand on this subject. "In the course of growing up, I expect you to try some things I wish you wouldn't. However, if you hide them from me, or if you lie to my face, I will feel hurt and angry. Being told the truth about what you do is more important to me than agreeing with all you do. I intend to hold both of us to honest account with each other so you keep me adequately informed about your actions and I keep you adequately informed about my opinions in response."

THE RISKS IN LYING

In general, adolescents tend to lie more than children. Why? Lies are usually told for freedom's sake. For many teenagers, lying seems to be the easy way out of trouble or into adventure that has been disallowed. But lying is deceptive: What seems simpler at the moment becomes complicated over time. The "easy way out" turns out to be extremely expensive, particularly for teenagers who have gotten so deep into lying that they have a hard time getting out.

For these young people, it can be helpful for parents to itemize the high cost of lying in order to encourage a return to truth. What to tell the errant teenager? Explain some of the common costs of lying.

- **Liars injure other people's feelings with the lies they tell.** Parents who are lied to can feel hurt because lies take advantage of their trust, can feel angry because of being deliberately misled, and can feel frightened because now they don't know what to believe.

- **Liars are punished twice.** If the teenager is found out, she is punished twice—first for the offense and second for lying about it.

- **Liars have to lead double lives.** Liars have to remember what they really did and the lie they told about what they did. Because they have two versions of reality to manage, telling lies proves twice as complicated as telling the truth.

- **Liars live in fear of discovery.** Concealing the truth, liars have to live in hiding. They start acting fugitively in the family, living in some degree of fear of being found out.

- **Liars become confused by all the lies they tell.** Covering up one lie with another, pretty soon liars lose track of all the lies they've told and find it harder and harder to keep their story straight.

- **Liars lower their opinion of themselves.** Each time they run from the truth, their self-esteem slides further down.

- **Liars become isolated.** To stay away from questions and to keep from being found out, liars distance themselves from family.

- **Liars believe their own lies.** What begins as lying to others ends up as lying to themselves as liars lose track of what really happened and come to believe some of the untruths they have told. Liars also lose intimacy with others.

Given so many costs of lying, why do children, and particularly teenagers in midadolescence, lie? Lying is generally done in order to gain illicit freedom, conceal a harmful truth, create a false impression, or avoid getting into trouble.

TEACHING YOUR TEEN NOT TO LIE

Parents should treat lying seriously. The quality of family life depends on the quality of communication, and lying can erode that quality to devastating effect. There is no trust without truth. There is no intimacy without honesty. There is no safety without sincerity.

So when your teenager lies, what can you do to help?

O Explain the high costs of lying so the child understands the risks that go with dishonesty.

O Declare how it feels to be lied to so the child understands how loving relationships can be emotionally affected by dishonesty.

O When your child has told a lie to someone outside of the family, close the loop of responsibility by making the child get back to the person lied to with a corrected version of the truth.

O Offer the child who impulsively or automatically lies a second chance to rethink the lie just told and correct it with the truth, no penalty attached.

When your child lies, tell her this: There are many compromises to be made in healthy relationships, but compromising about truth is not one of them. Without honesty, there can be no trust.

KEEP THE TRUST

In a healthy family, people trust each other to tell the truth. It is healthy for a parent to trust a child. It is healthy for a child to be trusted. It is healthy for that child to honor trust with truth.

When a child lies, treat that dishonesty as a major rule violation by applying some symbolic consequence (some task to be worked off) and then let the child know that hereafter you will trust in being told the truth. If your child keeps lying, you keep dealing with each incident as a major rule violation, applying some consequence, and afterward you keep reinstating trust. The message is, "In a healthy family, people can expect to trust each other's word, and that is the expectation to which you will be held."

Following these guidelines for discipline, you can get through your teen's midadolescent years with a minimum of pain and a maximum gain. Your child is growing up responsibly, thanks to your guidance.

Behavior Snapshot

It's normal for an adolescent to constantly push against all forms of authority to gain his freedom. And at some point in his rebellion he may even get into trouble. While you cannot make decisions for your child, you can give him your advice and experiences.

What happens: You learn that your teenage son has been involved in some vandalism with a group of other neighborhood boys.

What you *want* to do: Severely ground him. Clamp down. Deny him the freedoms that he seemed to be handling reasonably well.

What you should do: Go with him to the businesses affected by his behavior. Listen while he apologizes and makes arrangements for repairing the damage. Don't speak for him, but stay with him until the plan is clear for reparation. Go back after the work is done and see that it is satisfactory with the business owner.

Important Points to Consider

Midadolescence is often viewed as the period of childhood that is fraught with the most conflict. Here are some important considerations about discipline during this time:

O Midadolescents often live in the "now." As they navigate their way through this period, friendships and fun become more important than parental approval.

O While communication between parent and child does not always seem to flow naturally, keeping the door open, and consistently expressing this to your child, will help.

O Peer pressure has positive and negative attributes. As conscious parents, you have the ability to offer solutions and encourage your children to make choices that will benefit them in a positive way.

O Lying can cause a breakdown in relationships, which are built on trust. Model honest behavior and explain to your child the importance of not being dishonest.

 **CHAPTER 19**

Late Adolescence (Ages Fifteen to Eighteen) and Beyond

Late adolescence generally encompasses the high school years. As a high-schooler, your teen faces a new world. He may be awed by the size of the institution, intimidated by older and more experienced students, and excited by growth possibilities that did not exist before. His eagerness to catch up with what older students are able to do increases his desire for more independence. Remember, though, much of what is learned in high school is *outside* the classroom.

The Learning Curve of High School

Late adolescence ends for many young people with a mixture of triumph, loss, anxiety, and regret. There is triumph from knowing that one has actually completed high school. There is loss as one's community of friends begins to disband and disperse. There is anxiety about managing the next step into a larger world or job or further education. And there is regret that the simpler time of living at home and going to school is over, and now the true complexity of finding one's way in the world begins. It's a combination of heartbreak and triumph.

Late adolescence is all about learning to act like an adult. How does the teenager learn in high school? From direct experimentation with new and different experiences and from vicarious learning about the exploits of others.

FINDING A PLACE

Therefore, during high school, support ways that your child can associate socially with same-age friends. At the same time, so that he can get a social foothold, insist that your teenager join some extracurricular group that first year. Being on an entry-class athletic team or being in band, for example, can immediately provide a group to which he can belong. The more disconnected and lonely an entering student is, the more likely it is that he will be befriended by students already on the social fringe with adjustment problems of their own.

During the first year in high school, children need their parents' supervisory support to help them learn to live within school rules, join an organized student group, and keep up with the more challenging academic work.

GAINING INDEPENDENCE

During the high school years, three grown-up activities are now within your teenager's reach, each one of which empowers your son to act like an adult. His desire for more independence is dramatically increased, particularly if two or more of these conditions fire off at once. Now you have a more headstrong teenager to deal with than you had before.

What are these three rockets to independence, and why are they so powerful?

O Being old enough to drive a car causes the teenager to believe that this independent mobility means "I can come and go as I desire!"

O Being old enough to hold a part-time job causes the teenager to believe that earning independent income means "If I make my own money, then I can make my own choices!"

O Being old enough to socially date and party causes the teenager to believe that going out means "If I can go out and take someone out, then I can act socially grown-up."

Although parents want their teenager to be able to do all three adult activities, they want these new freedoms—because freedoms are what they are—to be kept within responsible bounds. Thus, you let your adolescent know he can do none of these activities without your permission, which you will give only as long as he is responsibly taking care of business at home, at school, and out in the world. What you don't want is for your teenager to combine all three grown-up freedoms into a lifestyle that takes over the young person's life. Thus, a part-time job pays for a car, a car enables dating, dating is expensive, and so more hours must be spent on the job. Who has time for chores or schoolwork now?

Driving a Car

Ask any teenager—a car is the "freedom machine." No longer dependent on parents to drive them where they want to go, when they want to go, being able to drive gives teens the freedom to "drive" their own lives. For the young person to rein in all that freedom so it is not abused to harmful cost to self or others takes enormous attention, judgment, and responsibility. It takes being reminded that a car is not a toy to have fun with; it is a transportation device for getting around. The best way for parents to consider whether they want their teenager to drive is to evaluate whether their daughter is mentally and emotionally equipped to manage the worst degree of risk that driving brings. This is the time for a frank discussion about sharing the costs of gas and insurance, especially if your teenager has a part-time job.

IS YOUR TEEN READY?

Parents should ask themselves, "In our judgment, is our teenager sufficiently mature to be entrusted with the freedom to use a complicated, and potential deadly, piece of equipment?" At worst, they are turning their teenager loose on the world with an instrument of destruction.

If their daughter shows signs of only being out for a good time and has a record of acting impulsively, heedless of consequences, parents should not allow this young person behind the wheel of a car. You should decide your teenager's readiness to drive based on how she is handling other aspects of her life.

THE TEEN'S RESPONSIBILITIES

You may hear arguments, because having this new freedom inspires desire for more. "What difference can two hours make, whether I'm in at midnight or at two? Nothing can happen to me at two that can't happen to me at twelve." Yes, it can. Consider the risk of accidents. The later your teenager stays out, the more likely she will encounter a drunk driver, or someone sleepy or asleep at the wheel. The later people stay up and stay out, the more likely substance use and fatigue will affect the choices they make. Continuing to allow your teenager to drive depends on her safe driving record. Any moving or other violations will cause you to re-evaluate. And any costs arising from such violations will be your teenager's to pay.

In general, having your teenager invest money she's earned to support some of the monthly financing payment (if you've bought her a car), insurance, maintenance, inspection fee, license fees, and gas that are all required for operating a car is helpful. Assuming part of these responsibilities can cause the teenager to appreciate how expensive this freedom is, and to drive carefully so more expenses from irresponsible driving are not incurred.

Holding a Part-Time Job

Entering the workforce can feel like an adult thing to do, and it is. Exchanging labor for money is what your child will be doing throughout his adult life. You want your son to learn the discipline of being able to secure and sustain employment.

There is much good experience your teen can gain from part-time employment. It takes initiative to find a job opening. It takes assertiveness to interview for a position. It takes responsibility to hold a job. It takes obedience to work for a boss. It takes cooperation to work with coworkers. And it takes patience to work with the public (which is what most entry-level jobs require a teenager to do). It also affirms self-worth to know that one has skills for which the world of work is willing to pay money. All of this is on the plus side of the ledger.

> Becoming a wage earner does not reduce the teenager's need for money to spend; it increases it. As income rises, so does the desire to do and have more things that he now wants to buy.

On the negative side of the ledger can be investing time at the job at the expense of education, because now making money feels more rewarding than making grades. Also negative can be what is learned from workplace associations—more access to substance use and other unwelcome worldly influences than existed before. Jobs can help teenagers grow up in a hurry as they work alongside older employees.

So parents must see part-time jobs for what they are—an opportunity for growth experience and possibly for harmful exposure. Their job is to monitor the mix so the good outweighs the bad. Since for many teenagers a cashed paycheck lasts about as long as a lit match, parents may also want to encourage the habit of saving—banking some part of the salary now for spending needs and wants later on.

The Teen Social Scene

Late adolescence is a time when dating becomes more common and partying becomes the socially grown-up thing to do. It is a time for the parent to keep a watchful interest in the activities of the teenager—not hovering or living through her vicariously, but being interested if a supportive conversation is needed.

GROUP SOCIALS

In general, dating initially makes teenagers feel awkward, anxious, even embarrassed. Going out with a group is usually more comfortable than going out with a single person. In addition, casual dating involves less pressure than serious dating. Casual dating tends to focus on fun without loss of freedom from significant involvement. Serious dating tends to focus on enjoying a single relationship and coming to know another person deeply and well.

When serious dating becomes exclusive dating, it can tie a teenager down and may be conducted at the expense of social time with other friends. Now the serious couple must manage tensions around mixing togetherness and separateness, and if infatuation develops, they must also manage tensions from possessiveness and jealousy. Loss of social freedom, distrust of commitment, and fear of betrayal can create discomfort when teenagers fall in love. For teens, being in love usually means being unhappy a lot of the time.

TEEN COUPLES

In general, most parents want to encourage low-pressure socializing—group and casual dating, keeping sufficient social freedom to have recreation time for other friends. If your teen gets seriously attached to someone, however, make sure you get to know her significant other. That will maximize your chance to influence the conduct of that relationship. If you oppose the relationship on the principle that they are "too young" to be serious, you risk driving them even closer together in response to your opposition.

Here are four questions for you to ask your teenager about the relationship. Yes answers to all of these indicates a respectful relationship.

○ **"Do you like how you treat yourself in the relationship?"** For example, she may like the freedom she gives herself to speak up, without any need for pretense.

○ **"Do you like how you treat the other person in the relationship?"** For example, she is open to hearing what the other person has to say, and she can listen when the two disagree without criticizing or correcting his point of view.

○ **"Do you like how you are treated in the relationship?"** For example, she may like how, even in conflicts, he never demeans her, and she appreciates never feeling pressured to do anything she doesn't want to do.

○ **"Does the other person like how you treat him in the relationship?"** For example, he may like how she is willing to listen, will compromise on decisions, and doesn't always have to get her way.

PARTIES

Parties can be a problem for teenagers because teens lack the social confidence and communication skills to meet and greet and chat with people they may or may not know. That's where the "get-to-know-you drug"— alcohol—comes in, providing the liquid courage to loosen up and feel less self-conscious about how one looks and what one says. Smoking cigarettes gives nervous hands something to do. Partying for the sake of partying can be very hard for many teenagers to do without the support of substances, particularly alcohol and cigarettes.

Attending a social get-together built around an activity or an event reduces the need for substance use. Now there is a planned focus for what everyone is there to do in order to have fun. Having social activities that have a purpose reduces social discomfort because it makes clear how everyone is to act. When you are hosting a party for your teenager, have plenty of activities available (and snacks for them to eat), in addition to announcing that it must be a substance-free occasion. This also means controlling the guest list, keeping a discreet but observable presence, and not allowing any crashers. If you want to know how to design a substance-free social get-together for teenagers, check with youth leaders at area churches. They do it successfully all the time.

Today, children experience pressures due to the Internet that most parents never dreamed of. Simply forbidding use will not prevent your child from the influence of social media. Keep an open dialog with your child about the pressures of social media and how it can lead to miscommunication, even between adults. Lay out your expectations for responsible social media use.

The Culture of Sex

In late adolescence, the pressures to have a complete sexual experience become more intense. Sex is used as a popular topic in entertainment and to sell a universal range of products. If advertisers can somehow find a way to make a product sexy, or associate it with a sexual image, it stands a better chance of enticing consumer interest. Sexual content is standard fare in TV shows, in print, and in songs. The media is filled with male and female sexual images and behavior.

Even more influential than the sexual images presented are the sexual roles that impressionable adolescents are groomed to play. Believe the images, and women are primarily supposed to be sexual attractors, trained to be preoccupied with their appearance to win male attention. Believe the images, and men are primarily supposed to be sexual aggressors, coached to act manly to win female admiration.

So what are you, as a parent, supposed to do to help your teenager grow beyond the restrictive sexual stereotypes the culture sends? Send more humanizing messages of your own. Let your daughter know that her value as a person is not limited to how beautiful she looks, and let your son know that his value as a person is not limited to how toughly he competes. And when it comes to socializing with the other sex, recommend that they aim for friendship first. Good friends tend to not get good friends into trouble sexually.

Use your parental intuition about a good time to discuss sexually transmitted diseases and birth control with your adolescent. You may find some helpful material at the library or local Planned Parenthood clinic if you feel a little shy about broaching these sensitive topics.

INTERNET AND SEXTING

Keep close tabs on your teenager's texting habits and note whether your teen is going over the line by sending or receiving nude pictures. This seemingly harmless personal flirtation can end up devastating a person's reputation if an image goes viral and becomes widely public. Monitor your adolescent's computer habits as much as you are able to. The combination of a web cam and computer in the privacy of his room might not be a good combination. Without constantly checking and violating his privacy, keep your finger on the pulse of what is going on with your teenager's digital expression of his sexuality. Teenagers often expect a certain level of privacy, and when it comes to the Internet, privacy is not always a sure thing. Discuss the potential consequences of sharing text messages and photos that the general public could potentially see.

Sexual Gaming

Growing up primarily in same-gender peer groups through elementary school and into middle school, girls tend to rely on each other for emotional support, sharing experiences and talking together, confiding to create intimacy. Girls are often socialized to base their self-esteem on their relationships. Boys tend to rely on each other for competition, sharing adventures and risk-taking together, testing themselves against each other to create companionship. Boys are often socialized to base their self-esteem on their performance.

By late adolescence, when there is more social and cultural pressure for sexual mixing, males and females can approach each other with very different motivations. A teenage girl may treat a boy as a relationship challenge, as a chance for social completeness—to get a boyfriend. A teenage boy may treat a girl as a performance challenge, as a chance for sexual conquest—to get a girl.

The more sexually exploitive a teenager acts, and the more she is sexually exploited by others, the more difficulty she will have establishing and maintaining a committed, loving intimacy later on in life.

Now begins the gaming to "get" each other in different ways. Some of the common stereotypes each has about the other at this age tell more of the story. For boys, girls are "all teases, out to tie you down." For girls, boys are "all hormones."

"True love" does not strike most teenagers in late adolescence, because of all the sexual gaming that gets in the way. Although sexual pressure is not all one-sided, it is more often aggressive male insistence that wears female resistance down. Sometimes a bad sexual bargain can be made. Insists the boy, "If you really loved me, you'd sleep with me," offering the lure of commitment in exchange for sex. Sometimes a girl feels something is wrong with her if she refuses. Insists the boy, "What's the matter, don't you care?"

Sometimes a boy, instead of taking no for an answer, treats it as a challenge to overcome, relentlessly keeping after a girl who, in his view, is playing hard to get. At last, the girl may give in just to get the pressure over. Then the word gets out. Boasting about his conquest, how he has "scored," the boy gets labeled as a "stud," while the girl is scorned as loose or easy and is called a "slut."

Given the sexual gaming that goes on in high school, parents need to encourage their late adolescents to be careful how they play. Tell your teenager gaming for sex just ends with someone, usually the girl, getting hurt.

Tell your son you don't want him pressuring, manipulating, or exploiting girls for sexual conquest.

Part of the parents' disciplinary job during their teenager's high school years is teaching their son or daughter how not to play the sexual gaming scene.

Romantic Relationships

Although starting a relationship with sex rarely leads teenagers into love, falling in love can often lead them into having sex as a physical affirmation and culmination of the emotional attachment they feel. One level of intimacy naturally leads to another, as all the love stories in all the movies they have ever seen have taught them to believe.

> Take the breakup of a teenage love relationship very seriously. Don't let a rejected boy—or girl—turn hurt from rejection into anger and try to retaliate. And make sure a rejected girl—or boy—does not slip from grief into self-destructive despondency from loss.

If your teenager is in a love relationship, he is much more likely to have sex. Therefore, if you see love blooming in your teenager's life, you definitely need to talk with him about what you wish for this relationship and about what you don't wish for this relationship. Besides the ordinary dangers of pregnancy and sexually transmitted disease, sexual activity between teenagers often brings them closer than their emotional intimacy can reach, and sex ends up frustrating, straining, and finally estranging the couple. Having sex only causes them to feel how emotionally far apart they really are. The best advice you can give them is to wait before having sex—wait and give themselves time to emotionally grow together, time to nourish their emotional attachment before they complicate it with sexual loving.

What to Say about Having Sex

Abstinence is one value many parents hold dear. Abstinence doesn't mean "not ever"; it means "not yet." It means delay, because the later an adolescent can wait to begin, the more judgment from maturity will govern decision-making and the less likely it is that harm will follow. It is worth advising teenagers that substance intoxication and sexual arousal are both mood- and mind-altering experiences—what seems wise is often not as compelling as what feels good. In both cases, impulse is encouraged, or allowed to take charge. When the two are combined, your teenager is much more likely to try sexual intercourse. Tell your teenager that the best way to prevent unwanted or problem sex is by staying sober.

> The most powerful preventions against premature sexual involvement in late-adolescent dating are true friendship for each other and maintaining chemical sobriety when together.

But suppose your teenager tells you that sometime this year, she is probably going to have sex. You can inform choice; you can't control it. You can't tie your teenager down or lock her up. Repeat why you do not believe it is in her best interests to have sex at this early age: It can confuse feelings, hurt self-image, complicate relationships, affect reputation, cause pregnancy, create parental responsibility, and transmit sexual disease. It may also be against your moral values or religious faith.

Then, give some guidelines for safely doing that which you do not want the teenager to do. "If you are determined to have sex, then have a plan so it is intentional and not accidental. Be sober and do it with a person you trust. Do not feel emotionally or physically forced or trapped. Be responsible and use protection. Do not feel exploitive or exploited. Do not assume that sex means love or love forever, and don't assume that love obligates you to have sex. Don't have sex unless you know that if the relationship ended, you would still feel good about yourself for having had sex. And do not feel that because you had sex once you are now bound to do it with this person or any other again."

Preparing for Independence

Once your child enters late adolescence (roughly coinciding with the entry into high school), you need to be thinking ahead to when high school is over. What happens next? Often this next step is going off to college or getting a job—in either case, probably moving out of the parents' home into shared living space with one or more roommates. This step will require more separation, freedom, independence, and responsibility than your teenager has known before.

Parents should try to encourage increased responsibility during the high school years so that the next step after high school feels as small as possible. New responsibilities will help the young person feel more prepared to function on his own. But how do parents teach this preparation? By teaching exit responsibilities and turning more responsibility over to their son during the high school years. It is helpful to your relationship with your adolescent to be very clear about finances—what you will pay for after he leaves home and what he should pay for. This clarity prevents resentment.

TEACHING EXIT RESPONSIBILITIES

At age fourteen or fifteen, or when your child starts high school, begin planning for graduation. By graduation, you want your teenager to be empowered with sufficient knowledge about responsible behavior and sufficient experience with taking responsibility to be willing and able to master the next step into more independent living. So freshman year in high school is the time for you to start thinking ahead.

The more exit responsibilities your teenager has mastered by the end of high school, the smaller and easier the next step into more independence will be.

Begin your teen's freshman year by asking yourself, "What exit responsibilities need to be in place at graduation to empower a successful transition into independence?" If you wait until senior year to ask these questions, you have waited too long. By then, with all the anxieties, distractions, and excitement that often accompany the final year in high school, a crash course in responsibility will not be well received by your teenager. Conflict, not learning, will result.

So, freshman year, list out the basic categories of responsibility in which your teenager will need competency to support more independence. The list is enormous. Then ask yourself the question "As the parent, at what point along the way through high school, and by what means, do I want to start teaching my teenager each of these responsibilities?"

From these objectives, you can back up and specify a rough sequence and schedule of preparation for teaching your child the significant responsibilities he will need to support more independence upon graduation from high school. For example, at what age do you want your child to start to manage a bank account, to balance a checkbook, to use a debit card, to be responsible for budgeting to cover routine expenses, and to save for the unexpected? At what age do you want your child to learn how to do minimum maintenance on a car—changing a flat tire, changing and safely disposing of oil, diagnosing common motor problems? At what age do you want your child learning how to find and hold employment? This list goes on and on.

TURNING OVER MORE RESPONSIBILITY

The second part of laying the groundwork for more independence after graduation is turning more responsibility for self-regulation over to your teenager in high school. Consider some of the self-regulatory responsibilities you may want to turn over.

O Being responsible for earning some of his expense money

O Managing household needs such as food shopping, cooking, cleaning, and laundry

O Being responsible for budgeting a monthly allowance that covers certain basic living expenses (phone, gas, clothing, lunch, for example)

- Managing homework and school performance

- Managing basic maintenance of a car (if driving)

- Managing social schedule, curfew, and rest

These and other responsibilities need to be progressively turned over so that by senior year, you have approximated full freedom of responsibility while your teenager is still at home. That way, should he fail in some area, you are still there to help him learn from mistakes. (Although these responsibilities are turned over while the teenager is still living at home, your son still must keep you adequately informed and contribute labor as part of his household membership requirements.)

Trial Independence (Ages Eighteen to Twenty-Three)

The last phase of adolescence, trial independence (from after high school through the mid-twenties), is in some ways the most challenging for both young person and parents. A young person faces considerable demands while finding her footing as a more independent person in a large and complex world. Living away from home for the first time, getting a job or going to college, sharing living space with a roommate, and being accountable for managing expenses all add up to more social freedom and responsibility than she has probably had before.

Parents are often still supplying some support but having less influence over, and more ignorance about, their young person than they had before. "Letting go" may make parents feel helpless and scared. And their fears are not unfounded.

THE RISKS OF TRIAL INDEPENDENCE

Most young people in trial independence do not find their independent footing right away. Lacking sufficient experience and responsibility, they slip and slide, breaking all kinds of commitments—financial, rental, legal, occupational, educational, and personal, among others—driving down self-esteem in the process. "What's the matter with me? I'm twenty years old, I keep messing up, and I can't get my life together!"

In addition, they may have no clear direction in life, no job path into the future they want to follow. "I don't know what I want to do!" Anxieties abound in the face of challenges posed by independence. To make matters worse, they are surrounded by a cohort of peers who are mostly feeling and acting the same, often escaping frustration and a sense of failure by partying. As this period of maximum alcohol and drug use begins, more dangerous drugs appear.

Lifestyle stress is common at this age. Your college-age child faces:

○ Sleep deprivation from late-night living

○ Lack of adequate nutrition from a snack-food diet

○ Debt from overspending

○ Deadline pressure from leaving demands until the last minute

○ Social loneliness when alone and insecurity in groups

○ Aimlessness from lack of goals

It's no wonder that at this age, some young people are susceptible to despondency, anxiety, exhaustion, and substance abuse.

FROM MANAGING TO MENTORING

A disciplinary shift is now required of parents if they want to help their daughter navigate this final and most challenging period of adolescence. They must give up the management strategies (with the exception of acceptance and affirmation) described so far in this book. They must let go of all corrective discipline. They are no longer in the business of making decisions for their child or bending the conduct of her life to their will.

The disciplinary power that parents can now provide is mentoring, not managing. You can offer counsel and instruction as a mature source of life experience that your young person can freely come to for support, understanding, and advice when the going gets tough.

As mentors, you should not tell your daughter what to do or "make" her do anything. You should not express disappointment, criticism, frustration, anger, worry, or despair. Instead, listen empathetically, advise if asked, let go of any responsibility for fixing whatever is going wrong, and offer faith that your young person, having chosen her way into trouble, has what it takes to choose her way out. You are respectful, constant, and loving.

Do not abandon your adolescent during trial independence. She's outgrown your corrective discipline, but she still needs your instruction. She needs you as a mentor.

If your daughter, having failed to find independent footing out in the larger world, needs to come back home for a short while, support this decision on a mutually agreed upon, limited-time basis. You should agree to this return so that your daughter can have a safe place and a simplified time to rethink, recover, and then re-enter the world to try independence again.

As mentors, experienced with your own trial-and-error education in life, you help the young person sort out what went well, what went awry, and what might work better next time. Let your daughter know that mistakes are one foundation for learning, and the only real failure in life is the failure to keep on trying.

Behavior Snapshot

As your teen enters late adolescence he is on the verge of independence. He has begun to taste independence through being able to drive, getting a part-time job, and dating.

What happens: Your teenage son wants to move out of the house, share an apartment with two friends, and drop out of high school so he can work more hours.

What you *want* to do: Absolutely forbid it. Shout at him that he's ruining his life—he'll never be able to accomplish anything without at least a high school education.

What you should do: Enlist the help of your partner; have a calm family discussion during which you help your son see the long-term ramifications of his actions; realize that ultimately the decision is his, as well as living through the consequences. Reassure him of your continuing love, even if you might not approve of his decisions and actions.

Important Points to Consider

Late adolescence is a time to focus on preparation for adulthood; however, this doesn't mean that your role as a parent is diminished in any way.

- As children enter high school, encourage them to develop healthy social relationships through positive activities.

- Teenagers in our society are surrounded by images and pressures related to sex. Having open and honest discussions about sex will allow you to encourage views that are not destructive.

- As your child prepares for adulthood, your role as a parent will shift from supervisory to consultative.

APPENDIX A

Helpful Websites

http://csefel.vanderbilt.edu
Center on the Social and Emotional Foundations for Early Learning (CSEFEL). Provides information and learning modules on nurturing emotional development during early childhood. The curriculum is available on the site, along with other resources that teachers and parents can look at or print.

http://challengingbehavior.org
Technical Assistance Center on Social Emotional Intervention for Young Children (TACSEI). A partner site to the CSEFEL resource. The two sites have a lot of the same resources. The strategy promoted is called Positive Behavior Support, or PBS.

www.OnlyChild.com
Information on parenting an only child.

www.drugstrategies.com
Guidance on effective drug treatment programs.

www.carlpickhardt.com
Monthly articles about parenting by author/psychologist Carl E. Pickhardt, PhD.

www.stepfamilies.info
Information about step relationships from the National Stepfamily Resource Center.

www.parentswithoutpartners.org
Information about single parenting.

www.FamilyEducation.com
Information about a wide range of parenting topics.

http://npen.org
National Parenting Education Network (NPEN). Research-based information about parenting and education.

http://parenting-ed.org
Center for Effective Parenting (CEP). For information about effective parenting.

www.tnpc.com
The National Parenting Center. Information from a variety of parenting experts.

http://pocketparent.com
This site features Gail Reichlin and her book *The Pocket Parent*. It has information for parents of children ages two through six.

www.thesuccessfulparent.com
Information about parenting adolescents and raising strong, resilient children. In addition to information on parenting adolescents, it has tips on education, temperament, siblings, and children and stress.

www.parents-talk.com
Expert advice and message boards covering a variety of parenting issues.

 **APPENDIX B**

Additional Resources

FURTHER READING

Bowers, Ellen, PhD. *The Everything® Guide to Raising a Toddler* (Avon, MA: Adams Media, 2011).

Holt, John. *How Children Fail* (New York: Perseus Books, 1964, 1982).

Holt, John. *How Children Learn* (Cambridge, MA: Da Capo Press, 1967, 1983).

Lickona, Thomas, PhD. *Raising Good Children: From Birth Through the Teenage Years* (New York: Bantam Books, 1994).

Lutz, Ericka. *The Complete Idiot's Guide to a Well-Behaved Child* (New York: Alpha Books, 1999).

Maslow, Abraham. *The Farther Reaches of Human Nature* (New York: Arkana, 1993).

Miller, Alice. *The Drama of the Gifted Child: The Search for the True Self* (New York: Basic Books, 1997).

Nelsen, Jane, EdD. *Positive Discipline* (New York: Ballantine Books, 1996).

Nelson, Gerald E., MD. *Good Discipline, Good Kids* (Avon, MA: Adams Media, 2000).

Pickhardt, Carl, PhD. *Keys to Developing Your Child's Self-Esteem* (New York: Barron's, 2000).

Pickhardt, Carl, PhD. *Keys to Raising a Drug-Free Child* (New York: Barron's, 1999).

Pickhardt, Carl, PhD. *Keys to Successful Stepfathering* (New York: Barron's, 1997).

Pickhardt, C.E. *The Case of the Scary Divorce: A Professor Jackson Skye Mystery* (Washington, DC: Magination Press, The American Psychological Association, 1997).

SUPPORT GROUPS

Parents Anonymous

http://parentsanonymous.org
909-621-6184
Strengthening families, breaking the cycle of abuse, and helping parents create safe homes for their children.

Al-Anon Family Groups

www.al-anonfamilygroups.org
757-563-1600
Helping families recover from a family member's problem drinking.

Index